CULTURE SMART!

SRI LANKA

Emma Boyle

·K·U·P·E·R·A·R·D·

T0019588

ISBN 978 1 85733 885 0

British Library Cataloguing in Publication Data
A CIP catalogue entry for this book is available from the
British Library

First published in Great Britain
by Kuperard, an imprint of Bravo Ltd
59 Hutton Grove, London N12 8DS
Tel: +44 (0) 20 8446 2440   Fax: +44 (0) 20 8446 2441
www.culturesmart.co.uk
Inquiries: sales@kuperard.co.uk

Series Editor Geoffrey Chesler
Design Bobby Birchall

Printed in India

About the Author

EMMA BOYLE is a British travel writer and author who has lived in Sri Lanka since 2003. After graduating in Philosophy and Politics from Liverpool University, she traveled extensively before finally settling in Sri Lanka. Her work has appeared internationally in publications such as *Conde Nast Traveller, Guardian Travel, Get Lost, Suitcase,* and numerous inflight magazines. As a contributor to hotel and villa reviews for boutique travel companies such as i-escape.com and Mr. and Mrs. Smith, her work has taken her across the world. She has also contributed to a number of Rough Guide titles, including *The Rough Guide to Sri Lanka* (2016).

The Culture Smart! series is continuing to expand. All Culture Smart! guides are available as e-books, and many as audio books. For the latest titles visit

www.culturesmart.co.uk

The publishers would like to thank **CultureSmart!**Consulting for its help in researching and developing the concept for this series.

CultureSmart!Consulting creates tailor-made seminars and consultancy programs to meet a wide range of corporate, public-sector, and individual needs. Whether delivering courses on multicultural team building in the USA, preparing Chinese engineers for a posting in Europe, training call-center staff in India, or raising the awareness of police forces to the needs of diverse ethnic communities, it provides essential, practical, and powerful skills worldwide to an increasingly international workforce.

For details, visit www.culturesmartconsulting.com

CultureSmart!Consulting and **CultureSmart!** guides have both contributed to and featured regularly in the weekly travel program "Fast Track" on BBC World TV.

contents

contents

Map of Sri Lanka

introduction

The pearl of the Indian Ocean; the land of serendipity; Taprobane: Sri Lanka has been known by various evocative names over the centuries, and has been fought over and freed from many an invading power intent on controlling the island's rich natural resources and advantageous geographical position. The influences of foreign powers, especially the Portuguese, Dutch, and British colonialists, have enriched Sri Lankan culture and are ever visible.

Sri Lanka's crushing twenty-six-year civil war ended in 2009, and the country feels positive in this new era of peace—the nation is developing, tourism is booming, and people are beginning to prosper. While it will take years for the scars of the conflict to completely disappear, Sri Lankan people are resilient. They have learned to live and work harmoniously alongside one another even during the darkest of times.

Sri Lanka is one of the world's great holiday hot spots and since the end of the civil war its tourism industry has seen huge expansion. The country continues to welcome increasing numbers of visitors year-on-year, drawn to the island's golden beaches, diverse wildlife, tea fields, mountains, and its eight World Heritage Sites, which include colonial forts, Buddhist temples, ancient cities, and forest reserves.

Urban centers are characterized by progressive development, multinational businesses, and

a competitive telecommunications market.
The pace of change in rural areas, however, is
typically much slower, and so entrenched cultural
traditions remain well preserved.

Sri Lanka shares many attributes with its South
Asian neighbors, but the fact of its having one of
the highest literacy rates in the region has resulted
in a politically conscious, interested, and engaging
people who take great pride in their country. Sri
Lankans are genuinely friendly, welcoming, and
curious people who take great pleasure in meeting
and hosting Westerners who respect their culture
and traditions. Loyalty is highly valued, and true
relationships are considered more important than
time or money.

Culture Smart! Sri Lanka outlines the country's
diverse and complex history, and unearths
the forces that have shaped its sensibility and
development over the years. It considers the
multiethnic character of the country, and by
touching on every aspect of life explains how
this has formed the values and attitudes of the
people. Offering an insight into how Sri Lankans
interact with each other, both at home and in the
workplace, and relating what they like to do and
where they like to go, this book will enrich your
visit to the island. Whether you come for business
or for pleasure, you are sure to have a meaningful
and memorable stay.

Key Facts

Official Name	Democratic Socialist Republic of Sri Lanka	
Capital City	Colombo. Population 753,000 (2018 est.)	Legislative capital: Sri Jayewardenepura Kotte
Main Cities	Kandy, Matara, Galle	
Area	25,332 sq. miles (65,610 sq. km). Similar in area to West Virginia	
Climate	Tropical monsoon. November–February: northeast monsoon. May–October: southwest monsoon. Heavy rain showers interspersed with periods of sunshine	The Hill Country has year-round rainfall. Temps. vary with altitude.
Land Use	Three-quarters of pop. live in rural villages; many are farmers. Arable land 21%; permanent crops 16%; protected parks and reserves 29%; other 34%	Produce incls. tea, rice, sugar cane, coconuts, spices, rubber, grains, precious stones, and fish.
Currency	Sri Lankan Rupee (LKR) At time of writing US $1 = LKR 179 1 GBP = LKR 226	The rupee is made up of 100 cents. One lakh = 100,000 rupees. The highest note is LKR 2,000.
Population	22,409,381 (2018 est.)	
Ethnic Makeup	Sinhalese 75%; Sri Lankan Tamils 11%; Muslim 9%; Indian Tamils 4%; others (e.g. Veddah, Burgher, Malay) 1%	

Age Structure	0–14 years 24% 15–64 years 66.3% 65+ years 9.7%	
Religion	Buddhists 70.2% Hindus 12.6% Muslims 9.7% Christians 7.4% Other 0.1%	
Languages	Sinhala and Tamil are the official languages.	English is spoken by about 10% of the population.
Government	The seat of government is in Colombo. The Executive President, elected for a five-year term, appoints his deputy, the Prime Minister.	Unicameral parliament of 225 members. There are nine administrative districts.
Media	Both private and state owned. TV and radio programs are in Sinhala, Tamil, and English.	Commercial stations include satellite and cable.
Media: English Language	Newspapers include *The Mirror*, *The Island*, *The Nation*, and *The Daily News*. Also, *The Sunday Leader* and *The Sunday Times*	
Electricity	230 volts, 50 Hz	Plugs have three round or square prongs.
Video/TV	PAL system	
Internet Domain	.lk	
Telephone	The country code for Sri Lanka is 94	To dial out: 00 + country code
Time Zone	GMT + 5.5 hours (winter), GMT + 4.5 hours (summer)	

chapter one

LAND & PEOPLE

GEOGRAPHY

Evocatively shaped like a teardrop, the island of Sri Lanka is situated in the Indian Ocean just twenty miles off the southern tip of India. Separated to the west by the Gulf of Mannar and to the north by the Palk Strait, Sri Lanka's only connection to India is a broken chain of limestone islands known as Adam's Bridge. With a surface area of 25,332 square miles (65,610 sq. km), Sri Lanka is similar in area to West Virginia, slightly smaller than Ireland, and twice the size of Belgium. It has a scenic 833-mile (1,340-km)

coastline, and the northeastern port of Trincomalee is one of the largest and safest natural harbors in the world.

Sri Lanka packs a surprising variety of natural attractions within its humble physical proportions, having rolling plains, mountains, plateaus, rivers, jungle, rain forests, lagoons, and coastline, along with two distinct zones based on rainfall: the tropical "wet zone" (southwest) and the extensive "dry zone" (north and east).

The island's topographical features can be placed into three categories distinguishable by elevation: the coastal belt, the plains, and the mountains of the Central Highlands. While the general terrain is mostly low and flat, interspersed with rocky outcrops that reach no more than a thousand feet, the hills and mountain peaks of the south central province reach elevations of more than 6,500 feet (1,981 m). Although Pidurutalagala (8,278 ft, or 2,523 m) is Sri Lanka's highest mountain, Sri Pada, or Adam's Peak (7,356 ft, or 2,242 m), a popular pilgrimage spot, is much better known.

The majority of the island's rivers have their source in the Central Highlands (the "Hill

Country") and flow in a radial pattern toward the sea. Only sixteen rivers are more than 60 miles (97 km) long; at 208 miles (335 km) the Mahaweli Ganga is the longest. In the north, east, and southeast the (often seasonal) rivers feed numerous artificial lakes, ancient tanks, or reservoirs, which store water during the dry season. The flow of some of the larger rivers has been artificially controlled in order to create hydroelectric, irrigation, and transportation projects.

CLIMATE

With monsoons occurring on opposite sides of the island at opposing times of the year, and as a result of the elevated altitudes of the Hill Country, Sri Lanka's climate is quite complex. However, since there is always somewhere on the island experiencing dry and sunny weather, the country attracts tourists year-round. Its position close to the equator means that the country enjoys a consistently warm climate with temperatures in the coastal and lowland regions averaging around 82–86°F (28–30°C) year-round. At times it feels much hotter, especially in the southwest "wet zone," since humidity levels can reach 90 percent. In the hills the story is quite different, since with altitude come lower temperatures; the daily average in Nuwara Eliya, Sri Lanka's highest town, is a fresher 64°F (17°C), and some nights are even cold enough for frost.

The months of May to September see the southwest monsoon bring wind and moisture from the Indian Ocean to drop heavy rain over the southwestern region of the country, while from October to March the northeast monsoon hits the east coast less severely. At this time occur frequent thunderstorms and heavy rains interspersed with sunshine that often results in flash flooding. The Hill Country, although affected predominantly by the southwest monsoon, typically sees a lot of rainfall year-round. Sri Lanka's "dry zone," located to the east and north of the island, sees far less rainfall—an annual average of about 59 inches (1,500 mm), compared to 98 inches (2,500 mm) in the wet zone—and most of this occurs only during the monsoon period.

THE PEOPLE

Sri Lanka has a population of more than 22 million, approximately 20 percent of whom live in cities. Most Sri Lankans belong to one of four ethnic groups identified by their language, their religion, or both: the Sinhalese, the Tamils, the Muslims, and the Burghers. The Veddahs make up a tiny fraction of the total population alongside more recent European settlers.

The Sinhalese

The Sinhalese speak Sinhala, and comprise around 75 percent of the population. Almost entirely bound together through their common belief in Theravada Buddhism, their language and shared heritage set them apart from their Tamil and Muslim neighbors. Forming the majority in most districts throughout the island except in the Tamil homeland of the north and the east, the Sinhalese are most densely concentrated in the south and west of the island.

The Tamils

While all Tamils are united by their common language, they are divided into two very distinct groups—the Sri Lankan Tamils and the Indian Tamils. In addition, the two groups have further distinctions based on caste and dialect, as well as religion; while Hindus constitute the majority of

both Sri Lankan and Indian Tamils, a substantial number of each group follow Christianity.

The Sri Lankan Tamils are descendants of Dravidian (South Indian) settlers of the kingdoms of Anuradhapura and Jaffna, who arrived as long ago as the third century BCE. They comprise around 11 percent of the total population and make up majorities in the northern and eastern regions of the island.

The Indian Tamils, also called Hill Country Tamils, are descendants of laborers brought over by the British in the nineteenth century to work on the tea, coffee, and rubber estates. The Indian Tamils live mainly in the Central Hill Country, reflecting their strong relationship with the plantation industry, and comprise approximately 4 percent of the total population.

The Muslims

Forming the largest ethnic minority after the Tamils, the Muslims are followers of Islam, and preserve their own cultural heritage, having distinct sites of worship and social circles. Most are descendents of Arab traders who began to arrive in the eighth century. Sri Lankan Muslims speak a form of Tamil peppered with Arabic words, as well as Sinhala and English. Muslims make up 9.7 percent of the population, and, while not in the majority anywhere, they make up large minorities in the north and east.

The Malays are also Muslim. Originating in Southeast Asia, they are the descendants of soldiers, prisoners, and political exiles brought from Malaysia to Sri Lanka by the Dutch administration. They often speak a unique dialect of Malay in their homes.

The Burghers

The Burghers are a distinct ethnic group characterized by their European ancestry. When the Portuguese and Dutch came to Sri Lanka, many settled and intermarried with the local Sinhalese. The children of these unions could not claim citizenship either from the European country of their father or from the country of their birth, and the term "Burgher"—from the Dutch *Vrij Burgher*, meaning "free citizen"—was born.

As the most Westernized of the island's ethnic groups, Burghers typically speak English as their first language, and are mainly Christian. Most Burghers live in the cities—Colombo, Matara, and Galle—and can be identified by their recognizably European-sounding surnames, such as Jansz, De Silva, and Peiris.

The Veddahs

Also called the Wanniya-laeto (forest dwellers), the Veddahs are descendants of the original Neolithic

community in Sri Lanka that dates from at least 16,000 BCE. They are a matrilineal society living in small settlements in the eastern highlands, and maintain little contact with other Sri Lankan ethnic groups. However, little else of their ancient culture has been retained. The Veddahs are characterized by their native dress and a social hierarchy preserved by local chieftains.

A BRIEF HISTORY

While Sri Lanka's ancient past is characterized by frequent invasions, records of the island's early history are so colored by legend that it is often tricky to determine the true course of events. Certainly, until Buddhism arrived in the island under King Devanampiyatissa, accounts of its early history are based more on the myths and legends of the time than on verifiable historical facts. However, it's very clear that Sri Lanka has, since earliest times, been a multiethnic society.

Prehistory

It is thought that Sri Lanka may have been inhabited as far back as 125,000 BCE. While archaeological evidence of early patterns of settlement is slight, it is thought that the Veddahs are the only modern survivors of these prehistoric people. Traditionally hunter-gatherers who used simple stone tools to live off the island's rich natural bounty, Veddahs are believed to have existed on the island since 16,000 BCE, ten centuries before the proclaimed arrival of the Sinhalese and Tamils.

Prince Vijaya

Prince Vijaya and his Indo-Aryan contingent
from Northern India are the legendary founders
of the Sinhalese race, and their arrival prior to the
Dravidian (South Indian) Tamils in the third century
BCE has been the subject of much debate. According
to the *Mahavamsa*, a Buddhist chronicle of the
island's early history, Vijaya, exiled from his father's
kingdom, landed on the west coast of Sri Lanka—
about where Mannar is today—on the
same day as the Buddha gained enlightenment
in 483 BCE. The prince and his seven hundred
followers came ashore and settled in the river
valleys, where they were able to cultivate rice.
Slowly they made their way, through ingenious feats
of hydraulic engineering, to settle in the island's
dry northern plains. The largest of the evolving
settlements became known as Anuradhapura.

The Kingdom of Anuradhapura (377 BCE–933 CE)

According to legend, the kingdom of Anuradhapura
was founded in 377 BCE by Pandukabhaya, the fourth
king of the Vijaya dynasty; however, it is for the time
of King Devanampiyatissa (300–260 BCE) that the
early Anuradhapura period is most significant,
since it saw the arrival in Sri Lanka of Buddhism.
According to the *Mahavamsa*, Mahinda, the son
of the mighty Emperor Asoka of India, arrived in
Sri Lanka in around 246 BCE with a contingent of
Buddhist monks, who quickly converted the King
and later the entire Sinhalese population to
Buddhism.

Buddhism essentially gave the Sinhalese their
national identity. Devanampiyatissa established the

the monastery of Mahavihara—the historic center
of Theravada Buddhism—and united Buddhism
with the political state. In the first century CE the
development of written scriptures gave the Sinhalese
a literary tradition, while the arrival of the Buddha's
tooth relic in 371 CE became not only a religious
symbol but also a symbol of sovereignty, since it was
believed that whoever was in possession of the relic
had the right to rule the island. Over a short period,
Buddhism achieved a divine status that quickly came
to be regarded as the highest expression of Sinhalese
culture.

Dutugemunu (161–37 BCE)
Sri Lanka's close proximity to India made it a
constant target of invasion. Successful attempts
would result in a handful of Tamil kings reaching
the throne at Anuradhapura—the longest serving
of whom was Elara, a general who arrived around

205 BCE and ruled the kingdom for forty-four years. During this period there were other settlements outside Anuradhapura ruled by minor kings and chiefs, the largest of which was Mahagama (modern Tissamaharama). From this kingdom came the famous warrior-prince-turned-Buddhist-king Dutugemunu (161-37 BCE), who made it his life's ambition to defeat Elara, eventually succeeding after a fifteen-year campaign. Having battled his way through each minor kingdom on his way to Anuradhapura, Dutugemunu united the whole of Sri Lanka for the first time.

Successive kings were unable to preserve the unity achieved by Dutugemunu, and long periods of instability, periods of Tamil rule, and Indian invasions were to shape the events to come. By the fifth century CE Tamil influence in Sinhalese affairs was growing, due to the increasing reliance that Sinhalese kings placed on recruiting Tamil mercenaries to support them in their own internal disputes. Hinduism in India was experiencing a revival, and a Tamil identity in Sri Lanka was beginning to emerge. In the end, it was the Chola— an ancient South Indian Tamil kingdom—that brought about the downfall of Anuradhapura when they sacked the city in 993 CE.

Polonnaruwa Kingdom (933–1255 CE)

The Cholas made their capital at the strategically defensible Polonnaruwa, sixty-two miles (100 km) to the southeast, and ruled the island from India for seventy-five years. Purely for symbolic reasons, the Sinhalese kings remained in Anuradhapura, however the frustration of repeated invasions eventually spurred the Sinhalese king Vijayabahu I (1070–1110 CE) to drive out the Cholas from Sri Lanka, capturing Polonnaruwa in the process. He reigned for forty years, and during this time succeeded in restoring many Buddhist temples and monasteries that had been neglected under Chola rule.

Vijayabahu died without an heir, and government was unstable until the advent of Parakramabahu I (1153–86), one of the country's most famous kings. Ambitious, indulgent, and a great patron of Buddhism, he launched a naval expedition against the Pandyas (an ancient South Indian Tamil kingdom that had defeated the Cholas) and Burma, and left a legacy of construction in the capital and island-wide reservoir-building that seriously depleted the royal treasury.

After Parakramabahu's death, the throne passed to his Tamil brother-in-law Nissankamalla (1186–96), who reigned peacefully for a decade before disunity and invasion prevailed, culminating in the terrorizing regime of Magha (1215–55) from Kalinga (a republic of central-eastern India), whose nonchalant attitude toward the upkeep of the capital contributed to its falling into disrepair. Gradually the population began to abandon the city to move further south.

The Kingdom of Jaffna

Even before the days of Polonnaruwa had drawn to a close, a kingdom was already beginning to emerge in the north of the country. Successive invasions by prominent South Indian Tamil empires, such as the Chola, Pandya, and Pallava, since the third century BCE, had consistently brought Dravidian settlers to the island and so weakened the Sinhalese kings that by the end of the thirteenth century they had retreated as far south as the Hill Country. By 1340 the Sinhalese monarchy split, causing two rival kings to establish themselves at Gampola and Dedigama.

As a result of the increasing fragmentation of the Sinhala kings, the Tamil kingdom of Jaffna in the north of the island flourished; Tamils seized control of the valuable pearl fisheries located in the Jaffna Peninsula, and established the town as an important center for the trade in elephants and spices. As waves of fresh migrants arrived, South Indian Hindu culture in Jaffna became firmly established.

This was to cause a division. As the Sinhalese retreated further south an ever widening gap separated the northern Tamil and southern Sinhalese settlements. This had severe cultural implications, since it effectively resulted in the creation of two distinct ethno-linguistic zones whose diverging cultures had different religions, influences, and traditions at their heart.

The Portuguese (1505–1658)
By 1400, there were three firmly established kingdoms on the island: the Tamil kingdom of Jaffna in the north, the Sinhalese kingdom of Kandy in the Central Highlands, and a new Sinhalese kingdom at Kotte, on the west coast of the island, near to present-day Colombo. Of the two Sinhalese kingdoms, it was Kotte—valued for its monopoly on the spice trade—that had emerged as the most powerful.

Recognizing the import of its spice—especially cinnamon—trade, the Sinhalese kings began to look toward foreign trade. So in 1505, when a Portuguese fleet was blown off course and landed on the west coast of Sri Lanka, it was warmly received by the King of Kotte, Parakramabahu IX (1484–1508), who invited the Portuguese to build a residence at Colombo for trading purposes. However, as the opportunity to exploit Sri Lanka's precious offerings grew, it soon became clear that Portuguese intentions were based on self-interest rather than on shared ideals.

Initially, the Portuguese were not interested in territorial gain—they did not have the manpower to support it—so they maintained good relations with the kings of Kotte. As their demands grew, however, relations soured, resulting in intermittent fighting that would continue until the death of King Rajasimha I (1581–93), when the Portuguese successfully annexed Kotte.

The Jaffna kingdom had, from the outset, remained hostile to the Portuguese, especially on account of their dogged determination to convert the Tamil Hindu population to Roman Catholicism. Despite King Kankili's (1616–19) furious massacre of the missionaries and their converts, Jaffna finally fell to the Portuguese in 1619. Only the independent kingdom of Kandy, which had aligned itself with the incoming Dutch, remained out of Portuguese reach.

The Dutch (1656–1798)

While the Portuguese were exploiting Sri Lanka's lucrative spice trade, the Dutch, already a dominating force in South Asia, were scheming to wrest control of this vital trade for themselves. They caught the attention of the Kandyan King Rajasimha II

(1635–87), who saw them as a means of ridding the island of the Portuguese. In 1638 an agreement was signed that gave the Dutch a monopoly on the island's major trade goods in exchange for Sri Lankan autonomy.

As the Dutch set to work on expelling the Portuguese, it soon became obvious that they were not intent on honoring their original agreement. While the eastern ports of Trincomalee and Batticaloa, captured in 1639, were handed back to the Sinhalese, the Dutch refused to hand over the strategic western ports of Galle and Negombo when they captured them the year after, thereby taking control of the island's richest spice lands. When the Portuguese finally surrendered Colombo to the Dutch in 1656 and Jaffna in 1658, the Netherlands had gained control of all of the island's coastal regions. The Dutch then effectively landlocked Kandy so that it would be unable to ally itself with another foreign power.

Having seized political control of the island, the Dutch concentrated mainly on the monopolization of trade, not only in spices but also in elephants, pearls, and betel nuts. Although efforts were made to impose the Reformed Calvinist faith on the population (declaring Roman Catholicism illegal), the Dutch were far more tolerant of indigenous religions than the Portuguese.

The British (1796–1948)

The French Revolution (1789–99) caused unlikely new relationships to be formed between the leading European powers. As a result, the Dutch permitted the British—who had been eyeing the strategic location of Trincomalee's harbor—to land in Sri Lanka in 1796 on condition that they would prevent it from falling into the hands of the Republican French. A further unspoken condition was that the British would eventually hand back control of the island to the Dutch. But this was not to be. Under the 1802 Treaty of Amiens, the Dutch part of the island became the Crown Colony of Ceylon.

By 1815, the British had also taken control of the inland kingdom of Kandy, becoming the first European power to do so, and the first rulers since Nissankamalla to bring the whole country under the control of a single power. Ironically, since the Kandyan kingdom had maintained its independence for so long, it was not by battle that the British took the city but as a result of disunity between disgruntled courtiers and their king, Sri Wickrama Rajasinha (1798–1815). As a result of Rajasinha's brutal suppression of the numerous conspiracies against him, courtiers and residents simply stood aside to let the British pass.

English now became the official language of government and, in order to open up the economy, all state monopolies were abolished. In 1832 changes in property laws made it easier for British settlers to buy land. This, combined with the sale of Crown lands, resulted in plantations springing up everywhere. While the British were initially interested in Sri Lanka only for her strategic naval importance, it soon became obvious that the development and trade of the island's own products could be of vital economic import too. Coffee production flourished, and from the 1830s to the 1870s there was a switch from the traditional reliance on subsistence crops to plantation agriculture. As a result, capital was quick to flow in.

In 1869 a devastating leaf blight was discovered, which destroyed almost all of the island's coffee crop within the next fifteen years. Fortunately, earlier experiments had shown that tea was well suited to the climes of the Hill Country and was soon to prove a more than adequate replacement. Rubber and coconut plantations were also flourishing. Since the British were unable to persuade the Sinhalese to work on the plantations, they imported a great number of Tamil workers as indentured laborers from South India, many of whose descendants continue to work on the plantations to this day.

The growth in the plantation industry paved the way for increased unity in the country, by way of the construction of roads linking the Hill Country plantations with the coastal ports. Railways were also established under the British and, along with hospitals, hydroelectric projects, and organized agricultural plantations, they provided the infrastructure for a viable national economy able to support its growing population.

The Rise of Nationalism

By the late nineteenth century a revival of Buddhist and Hindu movements led by individuals keen to preserve their culture in the face of repressive colonial rule was gaining strength. Prominent figures such as the Buddhist activist Angarika Dharmapala and the American theosophist Henry Steel Olcott—a Buddhist convert—helped to politicize the movement. In 1910, the declaration that a small electorate of Sri Lankans was permitted to send one member to the Legislative Council marked a minor victory, which set the ball rolling toward further change.

In 1919 the Ceylon National Council was formed to campaign for self-rule, and, as the movement grew larger and more organized, relentless lobbying for constitutional reform by united Sinhalese and Tamil organizations over the interwar years finally paid off. In 1931 the introduction of universal suffrage for an elective legislature and an executive council, in which power was shared with the British, gave the island's leaders the chance to gain political power with a view toward eventual self-governance.

Even so, during the Second World War the mainstream Sinhalese leadership collaborated closely with Britain, and Ceylon became Britain's front-line base against the Japanese.

Independence

In February 1948, Sri Lanka gained independence from Britain as "Ceylon," a dominion within the British Commonwealth. The first independent government was formed by the United National Party (UNP)—an essentially conservative coalition

that represented the island's major ethnic groups bound by the common ideals of Sri Lankan nationalism—under the leadership of Don Stephen Senanayake. For the first few years everything looked good: exports were doing well in world markets, the government had a significant majority in parliament, and there was little or no social unrest.

By the early 1950s, however, the situation had changed. Falling rubber and tea prices on the world market combined with high import prices resulted in increasing economic difficulties. The plantation Tamils suddenly found themselves disenfranchised by the UNP—an event that revealed for the first time serious fissures in the body politic based on a Sinhalese and Tamil ethnic divide. In 1951, the prominent nationalist S. W. R. D. Bandaranaike led his faction, the Sinhala Maha Sabha, out of the UNP to establish the Sri Lanka Freedom Party (SLFP).

The Bandaranaike Era

Since the 1956 general election coincided with the 2,500th anniversary of the Buddha's enlightenment and of the legendary arrival of the Sinhalese Prince Vijaya, the SLFP, under Bandaranaike's leadership, swept to victory on largely nationalistic grounds. The new government quickly passed the Sinhala

Only law, which, followed by the instigation of state support for Sinhalese–Buddhist culture, was to have lasting implications for a Tamil minority feeling increasingly threatened by the majority ethnic group. The growing tension would become politicized and lay the foundations for future Sinhalese–Tamil difficulties.

While the Bandaranaike government focused on policies of expanding the public sector and broadening domestic welfare, schemes restricting foreign investment and nationalizing critical industries and plantation land resulted in an inevitable slump in the economy and a growing feeling of discontent. While Bandaranaike was attempting in 1959 to bridge the growing ethnic divide by negotiating with Tamil leaders for a federalist solution he was assassinated by a militant Buddhist monk.

In the 1960 general election, the SLFP, under the leadership of Bandaranaike's widow, Sirimavo, swept to victory. Mrs. Bandaranaike, as she became known, became the world's first female prime minister. She continued broadly to follow her husband's policy of nationalizing key industries such as oil, while brutally enforcing the Sinhala Only law and deporting up to a million plantation Tamils back to India. Inevitably, ethnic tensions surfaced, and when riots broke out in the north and the east of the country she responded by curtailing Tamil political activity.

As discontent under the SLFP grew, the UNP triumphed in the 1965 general election. Declaring the economy to be virtually bankrupt, they attempted to create a mixed economy with an emphasis on the private sector, but with little success. By 1970 Mrs. Bandaranaike, head of a new SLFP coalition called the United Front, was elected back into government.

The Emergence of the JVP

The early 1970s saw the rise of the Sinhalese-Marxist People's Liberation Army (Janatha Vimukthi Peramuna, or JVP), led by Rohana Wijeweera. Its members were largely students and young men impatient for radical change and united in frustration at the lack of employment opportunities available to the growing populace. In 1971, as the JVP attempted to overthrow the Bandaranaike government, serious fighting broke out in central and southern rural districts and left many dead. The military quickly moved to suppress the movement and imprison its leaders as well as thousands of suspected insurgents.

This widespread unrest allowed the government to call for wider controls. In 1972 the constitution changed the country's name from Ceylon to the Democratic Socialist Republic of Sri Lanka. However, in the light of a declining economy and still rising unemployment the SLFP were resoundingly defeated by the UNP in the 1977 general election.

J. R. Jayawardene

Under the leadership of J. R. Jayawardene, the UNP reversed the Bandaranaikes' statist policies and established an open economy actively looking to attract back foreign investment. Initially, these policies showed some success: unemployment was halved by 1983, the country became virtually self-sufficient in rice by 1985, while tourism and expatriate Sri Lankans brought in an increasingly good supply of foreign exchange, especially in the face of growing inflation and unstable tea and rubber prices.

In 1978 Jayawardene introduced a new constitution, which handed over executive power to the president—a role that had previously been largely ceremonial. Resigning from his post as prime minister, Jayawardene became president in that same year and, after a few tweaks to the constitution, was reelected by popular vote in 1982.

The Civil War (1983-2009)

While relations between the Sinhalese and Tamils had been deteriorating since the 1950s, Tamil unrest had grown to irrecoverable proportions by the mid-1970s, due largely to their increasing alienation by the government; in legislation passed in 1971, the number of places available to Tamils in universities was cut, while a constitutional law decreed that Buddhism held the "foremost place" in Sri Lankan culture. Although Jayawardene's government made the concession of promoting Tamil as the "national language" of business in Tamil areas, this came too late.

As the Tamil cultural protest movement became increasingly politicized it also became violent as Tamil militant groups began to form. In 1976, a group of young people under the leadership of Velupillai Prabhakaran established the Liberation Tigers of Tamil Eelam (LTTE, or Tamil Tigers), which would become one of the deadliest terrorist groups in the world. Their goal was a separate state in the north and east of the island, which they called Eelam.

In 1983, growing tensions finally exploded. Tamil Tiger guerrillas ambushed and killed an army patrol in the Jaffna region, resulting in what was later to be dubbed Black July. In the week following the ambush Sinhalese mobs looted and killed Tamils island-wide, virtually leveling areas with large Tamil populations. It is not clear how many Tamils died in the atrocities; estimates vary between 400 and 3,000.

The fact that the government and security forces seemed unable to put a stop to the violence led many Tamils to flee overseas. Violence continued to erupt between the two sides and by 1985, despite the government's belated offer of limited Tamil self-government, security forces and the LTTE were engaged in skirmishes in the north and down the east coast. As a result, the country's economy took a nosedive as tourism slumped, foreign investment dried up, and military spending soared.

The Indian Peace Keeping Force

By 1987, government forces had isolated the LTTE in Jaffna City. Hoping to calm the situation, they had also signed an accord to create new councils for Tamil areas in the north and east. However, as fighting continued and thousands of displaced Tamils fled to the relative safety of Tamil Nadu's refugee camps in India, Jayawardene struck a deal with the Indian president, Rajiv Gandhi, to replace government troops with an Indian Peace Keeping Force (IPKF). By doing this, it was hoped to encourage the LTTE rebels to disarm and therefore return the north and the east of the country to peace.

In a short time it became apparent that this deal suited no one. While the LTTE was quiet for a time, frequent clashes with the IPKF soon resulted in an escalation into war. The LTTE was not the only group to oppose the deal; the Muslim quarter and the Sangha (community of Buddhist monks) voiced their disagreement, while Sinhalese nationalists—enraged that there was a foreign army on Sri Lankan soil—demanded that the IPKF leave, which they finally did in March 1990.

Return of the JVP

In 1987, as another wave of Sinhalese nationalism was ignited by the presence of the IPKF, the left-wing JVP exploited the opportunity to make a comeback. Inspired by communism and impatient for radical change, it proved to be more organized and more deadly than before. Still led by Rohana Wijeweera, it now included not only students and the unemployed but also monks, the police, and the army, who launched a series of attacks and political assassinations across the south and center that brought the terrified country virtually to a standstill.

In 1988, President Jayawardene was succeeded by a new UNP leader, Ramasinghe Premadasa, who defeated Mrs. Bandaranaike in the ensuing presidential election. As well as pledging to end the fighting with the LTTE in the north, Premadasa immediately implored the JVP to lay down their arms. When they refused he sent out paramilitary death squads designed to hunt down each and every member of the JVP leadership. By 1989 most of

the higher-ranking JVP activists, including Rohana
Wijeweera, had been killed or imprisoned, and the
rebellion was extinguished. While it is estimated
that tens of thousands of people were killed in the
insurrection, the JVP soon became, and remains
today, a part of the political mainstream.

The 1990s

Not long after the IPKF withdrawal, hostilities
between the LTTE and the Sri Lankan government
resumed. Most probably in retaliation for his part
in agreeing to Jayawardene's request to station the
IPKF in Sri Lanka, Rajiv Gandhi was assassinated
when an LTTE cadre member blew herself up in
front of him on his campaign trail in Tamil Nadu in
1991. President Premadasa was also the victim of a
suspected LTTE suicide bomber when he was killed
at a May Day rally in 1993.

In 1994 the leftist People's Alliance (PA)—a
coalition with the SLFP—won the parliamentary
election, thus ending seventeen years of UNP rule. Its
leader, Chandrika Bandaranaike Kumaratunga, the
daughter of the former Bandaranaike prime ministers,
became the country's first female president. Moving
well away from the SLFP's traditionally nationalistic
roots, Kumaratunga strove for economic liberalization
and national reconciliation with the aim of ending the
civil war.

Despite peace talks between the government and
the LTTE soon after Kumaratunga's election, the
conflict showed no signs of abating. As government
forces continued to attack LTTE positions, winning
Jaffna in 1995, the LTTE responded with more bombs,
the most notable targets of which were the Central

Bank in 1996, the Temple of the Tooth in Kandy in 1998, and the international airport in 2000. Just days before her successful presidential reelection in December 1999, Kumaratunga was also the target of a suicide bomber and narrowly escaped with the loss of her sight in one eye. Despite her successful election for a second term, Kumaratunga seemed unable to move toward a lasting peace.

Cease-Fire

Parliamentary elections were again held in 2001, resulting in the victory of the UNP under the leadership of Ranil Wickramasinghe. Kumaratunga remained as president. As prime minister, Wickramasinghe quickly moved to open negotiations with the LTTE, finally bringing them to the negotiating table, assisted by Norwegian peace monitors, to sign a cease-fire declaration in February 2002. Events moved quickly thereafter: weapons were decommissioned; the A9 road joining the Jaffna Peninsula to the rest of the island was reopened after twelve years; passenger flights to Jaffna were resumed; and the government lifted the ban on the LTTE. Most importantly, the LTTE surrendered its demand for an independent state in favor of a federal system.

At the beginning, hopes for a lasting peace looked positive. By the end of the year, however, relations between Kumaratunga and Wickramasinghe had soured to the extent that disagreements over the implementation of the peace process resulted in the LTTE's withdrawal from talks in April 2003. Later that year Kumaratunga used her powers to dissolve parliament (despite the UNP's having a mandate

THE TSUNAMI

On December 26, 2004, an earthquake off the Indonesian coast triggered a tsunami that brought devastation to nearby countries. Sri Lanka suffered heavily. Three-quarters of its coast was reduced to rubble; more than 30,000 lives were lost; millions of people were displaced; thousands of buildings were destroyed; half of the island's fishing fleet was washed away; and vital sections of road and railway line disappeared. The economic loss was huge: estimated damage stood at well over US $1 billion. In the face of this great tragedy, it seemed that the nation's differences might finally be resolved. However, as people struggled to cope, the government and the LTTE became embroiled in an argument over distribution of aid in Tiger-controlled areas.

When a controversial US $3 billion aid-sharing agreement, which allowed the LTTE to distribute aid to displaced people in the north and east, was ratified by parliament in June 2005, President Kumaratunga was criticized by JVP colleagues and Buddhist monks. Fiercely opposed to this agreement, which they believed would establish the LTTE as a de facto government in the north, the JVP walked out of the FA coalition—thus depriving it of its parliamentary majority— and then pressured the Supreme Court into suspending the agreement. In the end, and as Marxists protested across the island, Kumaratunga signed off the deal, despite holding a precious minority in parliament.

to govern until 2007) and call for an election. As a result of a new SLFP coalition with the JVP, Kumaratunga's Freedom Alliance (FA) narrowly achieved the majority it needed to defeat the UNP in the April 2004 parliamentary elections.

Meanwhile, the LTTE suffered setbacks of its own; many countries, including the USA, the UK, and later the EU, began listing the LTTE as a Foreign Terrorist Organization, while the LTTE's commander in the east, Colonel Karuna, broke away from the movement, taking several thousand troops with him. While Karuna fled underground, later to renounce terrorism and join the government as a member of parliament in 2008, the LTTE regained control of its eastern wing.

With the new prime minister, Mahinda Rajapakse, at the helm, the peace process stalled; violence in the east of the country between the LTTE, the Karuna faction, and the Sri Lanka military, combined with a suicide bomb in Colombo—the first since 2001—and the departure of the Norwegian mediators, undermined all confidence in the peace process. However, the economy, buoyed by high tourist numbers, continued to do well.

The Rajapaksa Era

In the November 2005 presidential election, widely thought to be one of the most crucial in Sri Lanka's history, the fiercely ambitious prime minister, Mahinda Rajapakse, narrowly triumphed over Ranil Wickramasinghe, the peace-oriented UNP leader who had brokered the original 2002 cease-fire. The election was boycotted by the LTTE, which forced people in Tiger-controlled areas not to vote. Although the LTTE's reasoning behind the boycott was not clear, Wickramasinghe was the preferred candidate of the minorities, so the loss of a potential 180,000 votes probably cost him the presidency.

When Rajapakse was sworn in as president, he vowed to continue peace talks with the LTTE. However, supported by the JVP and a party of Buddhist monks, he rejected the idea of Tamil autonomy and refused to share tsunami aid, initiating a confrontational anti-Tamil agenda.

As the first anniversary of the tsunami approached, world leaders, aid agencies, and the global community urged the government and the LTTE to end the postelection upsurge in violence and return to peace talks. Both parties agreed, and on February 22, 2006, peace talks were resumed in Geneva. While expectations were low, commitments to end the violence were made on both sides. However, these declarations lasted barely a month. By the end of March the Sri Lankan Navy and the LTTE were in conflict off the coast of Trincomalee. In April, when an LTTE suicide bomber in the main military compound in Colombo killed eight, the military launched air strikes on Tamil Tiger targets in the north, which forced tens of thousands of civilians to flee their homes. Further Sri Lankan Air force (SLA) attacks against LTTE targets in the north followed a mine attack on a crowded bus in Anuradhapura, which killed sixty-four civilians.

War had resumed in all but name as clashes, killings, bomb attacks, and fighting continued between the two sides throughout 2006. In October, as peace talks were set to resume in Geneva between the two sides, an LTTE suicide bomber killed over ninety sailors in a military convoy near Habarana. LTTE militants also attacked a naval base in Galle. As the Norwegian monitors continued to report repeated open violations of the truce by both the government and the Tamil Tiger rebels, it was clear that the cease-fire remained only in name.

March 2007 saw the Tamil Tigers reach new levels when they launched their first-ever air raid against a military base near the international airport. They followed this with another attack in July on an air force base in Anuradhapura, setting a new precedent in the long-running civil war. Hostilities continued to intensify, and by the end of the year the government had finally regained control of the Eastern Province.

In January 2008 the government announced its withdrawal from the 2002 cease-fire agreement with pledges to win the war within a year. Bomb attacks, political assassinations, disappearances, and heavy fighting in the north were to form the growing pattern of progress. When the LTTE offered a unilateral ceasefire, the response by hardline Defence Secretary Gotabhaya Rajapaksa, the President's brother, was a firm no, calling it a ploy by the LTTE to strengthen their position under the cover of negotiations.

By mid-2008, after recapturing Mannar on the west coast, the Sri Lanka Army entered The Vanni, the Tamil Tiger's last jungle stronghold and quickly ordered NGOs, UN agencies and foreign journalists to leave. Tamils were left without humanitarian support, and devoid of a human-rights watchdog, the increasing accusations of atrocities committed on both sides meant that claims would soon become impossible to verify.

Having captured Pooneryn at the end of 2008, the entire west coast of Sri Lanka was back under government control and a land route opened to Jaffna. By January 2009, the Sri Lankan Army had reached Kilinochi, the de facto LTTE capital, quickly followed by strategically important Elephant Pass and Mullativu, the last significant LTTE stronghold. As the SLA advanced further into The Vanni, remaining LTTE cadres, and with them, some 300,000 Tamil civilians, were forced into a tiny coastal area northeast of Mullaitivu.

The End of the War

Amid growing claims of a humanitarian crisis, the UN called for an immediate ceasefire. Although fighting continued, passages were opened to let civilians flee into so-called "no-fire zones", though even those were shelled by the SLA who accused the LTTE of launching attacks from within the safe zones and using civilians as human shields. Bombarded day and night, the LTTE's request for a ceasefire was once again rejected by Gotabhaya Rakapaksa, who saw the end of the civil war in sight.

What ensued was a bloodbath where thousands of Tamil civilians—possibly up to 30,000—were indiscriminately killed by both sides as they attempted to escape. Tiger forces blocked many from leaving in a final desperate attempt to hold their ground. By May, it was over. With the last LTTE fighters surrounded, they surrendered their weapons and admitted defeat. President Rajapaksa declared victory by announcing the death of Prabakaran, the LTTE's elusive rebel leader who had brought the battle to its bitter end.

Peace and the Postwar Years

Peace was welcome yet bittersweet. With thousands of beleaguered refugees interned in refugee camps, serious allegations of war crimes continued to be raised about the behavior of both sides during the final stages of the conflict, particularly the SLA's continued bombardment of Tamil civilians in no-fire zones and the post-surrender execution of senior LTTE figures and other civilians suspected of LTTE involvement. Continuing to refuse access to international mediators, the government set up its own reconciliation committee to address the claims, but this was largely seen to be a cover and anyone critical of the regime, particularly journalists, were often threatened and attacked.

In the years that followed, Rajapaksa (and his family, many of whom held key government ministries including the key ministries of defense and economic development) continued to consolidate his power with a presidential election victory in 2010 followed by a parliamentary victory against an opposition UNP led once again by Ranil Wickramasinghe. Among the inevitable constitutional amendments that followed, the two-year cap on the number of terms the president could serve was removed.

Even before the war had finished, the government had started ploughing millions of rupees into improving the country's infrastructure, creating new roads and repaving others, and building a second international airport and a Chinese-sponsored deep water port in Rajapaksa's home district of Hambantota. The government also reestablished and reopened the railway line north to Mannar and Jaffna.

A New Era

Mahinda Rajapaksa was defeated in the surprise early 2015 presidential elections by an unlikely candidate—his former cabinet colleague and close ally, the Health Minister, Maithripala Sirisena, who called for an end to the corrupt and nepotistic Rajapaksa regime. Backed by the UNP and many disparate minority factions whose main goal was to oust the Rajapaksas, a parliamentary victory followed, whereby Ranil Wickramasinghe was appointed once again as prime minister.

In the months that followed, Sirisena remained true to his election promises, amending the constitution to reduce presidential powers to two terms of office, and reconsolidating the powers of parliament and the judiciary. Media censorship was also lifted. The vast scale of the Rajapaksa corruption was also revealed, though few individuals were implicated. Much-needed development continues across the country, making up for years of lost time. Colombo—once a forlorn capital city—is now booming. Large swathes of the city are effectively construction sites as shiny new condominiums and shopping complexes remold the city's skyline, and independent cafés, restaurants, shops and galleries spring up everywhere.

While the country attempted to rebuild itself and prosper from a booming tourism economy, and look towards a much-deserved era of peace, the government failed to make progress. Sirisena's ambitious attempts at reform were constantly stymied by a coalition government he struggled to control, resulting in accusations of political inaction and frustration by the electorate.

In the local elections of February 2018, the Rajapaksa-dominated Podumaja Peramuna Party garnered the most votes, followed by Wickramasinghe's UNP party and President Sirisena's Sri Lanka Freedom Party. In November 2018, most SLFP MPs defected from the coalition

government, prompting President Sirisena to dissolve parliament and appoint a new cabinet led by Mahinda Rajapaska. This precipitated a constitutional crisis, with two parallel governments claiming legitimacy. In December, however, the Supreme Court ruled the dissolution of parliament unconstitutional. Rajapaksa stepped down and Wickramasinghe was reappointed prime minister.

GOVERNMENT AND POLITICS

Sri Lanka has a democratic government, with an executive president who is both head of state and head of government as well as commander-in-chief of the sizeable armed forces. While it gained independence from Britain in February 1948, the present constitution, which provides for an executive president based on the French model, was not adopted until August 1978. Despite the civil war, and high levels of political violence associated with the JVP during the 1980s, the government is relatively stable. No military coups or uprisings have toppled it during its existence.

The terms of the 1978 Constitution state that Sri Lanka is a Democratic Socialist Republic. All citizens are equal before the law, and in recognition of the pluralistic character of Sri Lankan society, no discrimination should be made on grounds of ethnicity, religion, language, or caste. The legal voting age is eighteen, and there are two official languages: Sinhala and Tamil.

Sri Lanka is divided into nine provinces, each of which have councils with legislative powers in the areas of education, health, rural development, social services, agriculture, and local taxation. Provincial councils are directly elected for a five-year term and the head of the council majority serves as chief minister. Beneath them are municipal, urban, and village councils.

The Executive

The president is involved in every aspect of government. Responsible to parliament for the exercise of duties under the constitution and laws, the president may be removed from office by a two-thirds majority in parliament with the agreement of the Supreme Court. The prime minister is appointed by the president from the ruling party, to be his deputy and head of cabinet.

In presidential elections, the winner must gain more than 50 percent of the public vote, and is qualified to serve a term of five years, which can be extended to a second term.

The Legislature

Sri Lanka has a unicameral legislature with 225 members, 196 of whom are directly elected through a system of modified proportional representation using a preferential method for a period of five years. The remaining 29 seats are allocated to other political parties and groups equal to their share of the national vote. Although the president has the power to summon, suspend, or end a legislative session, and dissolve parliament, parliament reserves the power to make laws and repeal or amend the constitution.

The Judiciary

The judiciary consists of the Supreme Court and the Court of Appeal, whose judges are appointed by the president and serve for a lifetime period (until 65 years old), as well as a High Court and a number of subordinate courts. Independent of the executive and the legislature, Sri Lanka's legal system reflects its history and diverse cultural influences. While criminal law remains fundamentally British, basic civil law is Roman-Dutch. Kandyan, Jaffna, and Muslim laws still retain substantial regional influence in personal disputes. Court cases in Sri Lanka, especially those in the lower courts pertaining to land disputes, can take years to resolve.

Foreign Relations

Sri Lanka has traditionally followed an internationally nonaligned foreign policy. It participates in multilateral diplomacy, particularly in the UN, with the aim of promoting sovereignty, independence, and development in the developing world. Sri Lanka was a founding member of the Non Aligned

Movement (NAM) and has remained a member of the Commonwealth since independence. It is also a member of the South Asian Association for Regional Cooperation (SAARC), the World Bank, the International Monetary Fund (IMF), and the Asian Development Bank (ADF).

THE ECONOMY

Sri Lanka is a middle-income country, with a per capita GDP of US $4,065 in 2017. Historically, the economy has been heavily dependent on agriculture, which employs just over a third of its eight-million-strong labor force. However, in recent years, thanks to a huge growth in the manufacturing and service sectors, the economy is now more urban-focused. Annual growth rates of around 5.8 percent in the postwar years reflect the island's firm commitment to development, though growth has slowed in recent years. Sri Lanka has always welcomed foreign trade; however tricky regulations and red tape mean the country attracts a much lower volume of Foreign Direct Investment (FDI) than neighboring countries.

Sri Lanka's social indicators rank among the highest in South Asia and compare with those in middle-income countries. Over the last decade, the government has made efforts to support domestic enterprise and reduce poverty, and ecent economic growth has also assisted in shared prosperity: The national poverty headcount ratio declined from 15.3 percent in 2006/07 to 4.1 percent in 2016. Extreme poverty in Sri Lanka is rare and confined to certain geographical areas, however a significant proportion of the population still hovers just above the extreme poverty line.

Today, Sri Lanka's most dynamic areas are tourism, textiles, apparel, tea exports, rice, port construction, and telecommunications. The services sector, which includes income from tourism, is the largest sector of the economy; it employs 45 percent of the total labor force and contributes roughly 62 percent of GDP. Its biggest exports are clothing, tea, cut diamonds, and jewelry, coconut products, rubber, and fish. Major imports include textile fabrics, mineral products, petroleum, foodstuffs, machinery, and transportation equipment. The USA, India, UK, Italy, and the UAE are some of Sri Lanka's largest trading partners.

Sri Lanka also relies heavily on foreign aid and the remittances of the more than 1.5 million Sri Lankans who live abroad (90 percent of whom live in the Middle East) and send home US $500 million every month.

VALUES & ATTITUDES

Sri Lanka shares many core values with other South Asian countries. Irrespective of religion or ethnicity, great importance is placed on the value of education; religion is a significant part of daily life; and family ties, tradition, and the community are held in high regard. Despite being defined by ethnicity, social background, and religion, Sri Lankans as individuals are united through a shared pride in their national identity. Many have put the pain of the civil war years firmly behind them and focus instead on fostering good relations with one another and rebuilding their future.

Like much of South Asia, Sri Lanka is a patriarchal society. However, as a result of the country's free

educational system and postindependence egalitarian social policies, Sri Lankan women have more advantages than their South Asian sisters. Literacy is almost universal, and while traditional attitudes remain, especially in rural areas, there is greater equality between the sexes at home and in the workplace, especially in comparison to Sri Lanka's closest neighbor, India.

CASTE AND CLASS

Sri Lankans are very aware of social order and status. As a result of the traditional caste system, social equality in rural areas may still be a novel concept to many Sri Lankans, even though it has seen national acceptance in the country's constitutional and legal framework. All relationships still involve hierarchies to some extent, even at the highest levels, although merit and achievement are beginning to outweigh caste and class.

The caste system played an important role in the island's rural society, where stratification occurred primarily as a result of the trade, craft, or profession a person was born into. Caste is hardly visible in society today, save for its influence in the marriage market.

Although Sri Lanka's social structure traditionally consisted of the rulers and the ruled, the nineteenth century saw the rise of the Sri Lankan middle class. In the seventeenth century the Portuguese had enlisted the support of and elevated people from other social groups in return for loyal service, thus creating the Mudaliyar caste, and it went on to flourish under the British colonial government. These Westernized, primarily urban professionals (lawyers, doctors, teachers, and skilled workers) competed with the traditional Sri Lankan elite to form a new class of achievers that transcended divisions of race and caste. When free education was introduced in 1944, followed by a focus on equality-based social welfare policies, it further became possible for achievers from all walks of life and of both sexes to transcend the class divide.

Sri Lankan society today is loosely split into three social groups: a small class of very wealthy urbanites, a growing middle class, further divided into an upper and lower level, and the rural poor. Sri Lankans typically socialize within their own groups (although exceptions occur), and there is an obvious division between the rich elite—identified by their command of English, education in exclusive schools and universities overseas, and expensive possessions—and the poor, nowhere more so than in Colombo, where wooden shacks sit alongside huge mansions. There are also further divisions based on the differing values of the urban and rural population.

RELIGION

Sri Lanka is multireligious; the Buddhist majority generally live peacefully beside sizeable Hindu, Muslim, and Christian communities. Intermarriage is increasingly common, and many individuals socialize together and share in the festivities of their friends' faiths, while major local events, such as the opening of a school, are often marked by representatives of each faith together. The value of religion to each ethnicity is equally important: they regularly practice their faith at home as part of the daily routine—lighting candles, praying—and try to live by its code of conduct. The festivities of each religion are woven deeply into the island's culture, and some pilgrimage sites are shared;

Kataragama is venerated by Muslims, Buddhists, and Hindus alike, while the famous footprint atop Adam's Peak is worshiped by all.

Buddhism

Dating from the third century BCE, Sri Lanka was one of the first countries in the world to adopt Buddhism, and it has always played a significant spiritual, cultural, and at times political role in the country. Sri Lanka is the preserver of some of Buddhism's most important scriptures, since it was here that the Buddha's teachings were first committed to writing in 30 BCE. Much of Sri Lanka's culture, in the form of painting, sculpture, and literature, is inspired by Buddhist ideals.

Theravada Buddhism—the embodiment of the Buddha's teachings, or *dharma,* in Pali (the ancient language of India derived from Sanskrit)—is most commonly practiced in Sri Lanka. The Buddha emphasized that each person is responsible for his or

her own spiritual welfare. The ultimate aim is to pass, through meditation and self-sacrifice, beyond the karmic cycle to reach the spiritual state of *nirvana*, where desire, suffering, and causality finally end. Pious devotees aim to improve their *karma* by following the philosophy of the Four Noble Truths and seeking the moral guidance of the Eightfold Path.

THE FOUR NOBLE TRUTHS
Life is suffering.
Suffering is the result of desire.
It is possible for suffering to cease.
The Noble Eightfold Path will lead to a release from suffering.

THE EIGHTFOLD PATH
Wisdom
• Right view • Right intention
Ethical Conduct
• Right speech • Right action • Right livelihood
Mental Development
• Right effort • Right mindfulness • Right concentration

Buddhism is an important part of daily life in Sri Lanka for around 70 percent of the population; Buddhist temples and the white domes of *dagobas* (stupas) characterize every town and village, while festivals are carried out with great vigor. *Poya* (full moon) days are of particular importance to Buddhists, and are official public holidays.

Since there is no form of organizational or congregational worship, devotees visit their local temples as they wish, lighting candles, making *puja* (prayers and offerings), reciting the *pirith* (Buddhist scriptures), and listening to the ancient truths. Although devotees often bring lotus flowers to offer to the Buddha, he is above all a teacher who provides guidance. Sri Lankan Buddhists also worship a select number of Hindu gods who they believe help them to achieve specific aspirations, such as success in a business enterprise, fertility, or fortune with the harvest. The shrines to these gods are called *devales*.

Hinduism

Approximately 13 percent of the population follow Hinduism. Devotees are mainly Tamils living in the north and east of the island, but there are also followers in Colombo, Kandy, and the tea plantations of the Hill Country. While it is thought that Hinduism was practiced on the island before the arrival of Buddhism, it was not until the later Anuradhapura and early Polonnaruwa periods that it became firmly established by successive Tamil kings.

Hinduism does not follow a book, nor does it have a single founder or religious structure. Despite there being innumerable deities, there is only one god at the heart of the religion—the infinite, formless Brahman. The many deities are actually manifestations of Brahman, and since they represent the many facets of life, such as wealth, fortune, and beauty, they allow people to reach God through many ways. Of the three highest manifestations (*Trimurti*) of Brahman, Siva is particularly venerated by Sri Lankan Tamils. Popular lesser deities include the elephant-headed Ganesh, the goddess of fertility, Pattini, and Kataragama, god of war.

Hinduism is a way of life: the fulfillment of ritual and social duties will enhance a devotee's *karma*. Sri Lankan Hindus often have pictures of their favorite deities in their homes, use idols and images in their daily worship, and regularly visit *devales* and *kovils* (Hindu temples).

Islam

Islam was founded in the seventh century CE by the Prophet Mohammed, and introduced to Sri Lanka a century later by descendants of Arab traders who settled on the island. Comprising 9 percent of the population, Muslims generally live in separate communities in order to preserve and practice their Islamic culture. Devotees of Islam, a monotheistic faith, pledge to surrender to the will of Allah (God) as revealed to Mohammed and recorded in the Koran.

Sri Lankan Muslims generally follow the Sunni school of Islamic law. The Five Pillars of Islam are: the *shahada*, or creed; prayer five times a day; fasting during Ramadan; almsgiving; and the Hajj, or pilgrimage to Mecca. Each Muslim community is built around a cupola-domed mosque, to which devotees are called five times a day to congregate and pray. The most spiritual day is Friday, when they go to the mosque to observe *Salat al-Jummah*, or Friday prayers.

Christianity

While some Christians believe that Thomas the Apostle was active in Sri Lanka in the first century CE, it was not until the advent of colonial rule that Christianity had a significant impact on the population. Catholicism, which comprises much of the 7 percent Christian community, remains strong in many western coastal towns and villages, including Colombo, Negombo (often known as "Little Rome") and Mannar, whose Our Lady of Madhu Church receives up to 300,000 pilgrims every August.

KARMA

Sri Lankans are more relaxed about missed opportunities than Westerners because they believe that if something does not work out it was not meant to be, and that it will probably come around again at a more opportune time, with more success. The cause of this attitude is the belief in *karma*—the cycle of cause and effect—where an individual's good or bad deeds determine his or her future. Both Buddhists and Hindus believe in reincarnation, and that good deeds in this life will improve one's position in the next, with the goal of eventually reaching a state of release from the cycle (*nirvana*).

For Buddhists, all karmic actions result from mental intent and must be genuine. Even if someone appears to be professing piety on the outside but underneath is doing something only for selfish reasons, eventually it will have a negative effect on a person's *karma* because it is the fundamental intention of the action that is key. To Buddhists, *karma* is not predetermined or fatalistic: people act of their own free will to create their own destiny.

THE FAMILY

The family is highly valued in Sri Lankan society, and is a source of great strength. Among all ethnicities both the nuclear family and the extended family are vitally important social units. The father is typically the head of the household, while women are responsible for the home and children, although the civil war has resulted in many widows having to take the dominant role. Older family members are valued more highly than in the West, and typically live with their adult children in old age. Nursing homes do exist, but are poorly funded and considered a last resort—usually when the family has insufficient funds or desire to look after their relations.

There is a strong sense of community in most families; those with good connections and those in a good financial position will often help in times of difficulty (or be expected to) and assist in finding even an unqualified member of the family a good job. So, for all the strengths that the extended family offers, there are also obligations and demands.

EDUCATION

Sri Lankans value education greatly as a means of improving one's prospects in life. At 92 percent, the country has one of the highest literacy rates in South Asia. While much of this can be attributed to the free education system that has been in place since 1944, the efforts of postindependence governments to make education from kindergarten to university level one of their highest priorities have contributed to a steady rise in literacy rates and educational attainment levels. The medium for instruction in schools is usually Sinhalese or Tamil, and sometimes English, depending on the locality.

Where possible, children attend Montessori or preschool classes before starting their education proper at the age of five years. Three sets of standardized exams from primary level until GCE (Ordinary Level) provide the children with plenty of work both at school and at home. Success in these can lead to subsequent educational privileges, so the children of parents who can afford it often attend private tutorial sessions in the afternoons in addition to their regular schooling, in the expectation that advancement in learning will also give them increased security for the future. In rural areas children may walk a few miles to school, and facilities and equipment can be poor. Schools are formal: teachers are respected as authority figures, and children wear smart white uniforms.

It is compulsory for children to attend school between the ages of five and thirteen, and after this they are strongly encouraged to stay on until at least the completion of their GCE (Ordinary Level) exams at the age of fifteen or sixteen, after which they can proceed to the higher (Advanced Level) exams to qualify for university entrance. However, due to the island's largely agrarian society, it is not surprising that more than a third leave early to help with work in the fields.

While government schools are generally coeducational, some of the most sought after institutions across the country are single-sex schools and entry to these is very competitive. Private schools and fee-paying international schools (some with British curriculums) are preferred by wealthier families.

University education is free; but competition for the limited number of places means that many qualified students miss out. Those who can't get into one of the fifteen state-funded universities may choose to continue their education abroad (an expensive option open to a privileged few), join the Sri Lanka Open University, or enroll in one of the state-owned degree-awarding institutes. Even after this, graduates still have difficulty in finding jobs.

THE URBAN-RURAL DIVIDE

By tradition, Sri Lanka is an agrarian society. Three-quarters of the population live in rural towns and villages (*gamma*) scattered throughout the island. The increasing numbers of Sri Lankans migrating to the cities for educational or employment opportunities still retain close ties with their rural home areas, and escape back there as often as they can. The richer urban population continues to grow increasingly Westernized in its standard and style of living, while the rural villages, especially the most isolated ones, are more likely to retain their traditional familial values and attitudes.

Sri Lankans living in rural areas are generally more conservative, certainly in dress and behavior, than most city dwellers. Village girls might have more traditional aspirations than their richer urban counterparts, looking forward to finding a suitable husband and starting a family rather than embarking on a high flying working career.

ATTITUDES TOWARD WOMEN

Sri Lankan society is still influenced by traditional patriarchal values, whereby women are respected more as mothers and homemakers than for the prestige of their job status. Clear distinctions, especially in rural areas, are still made in the roles of the sexes so that household work, raising children, and cooking are seen as women's work, while men are the providers and protectors of the family. However, as a consequence of the civil war and the 2004 tsunami, when over 30,000 Sri Lankans lost their lives, women now head more than one-fifth of

Sri Lankan households. A number of organizations offer support for women both in the workplace and at home.

Sri Lankan women are more fortunate than their Asian sisters, since their access to education and the subsequent high literacy rate has resulted in their having access to numerous economic opportunities unmatched in other Asian countries. State-funded schooling removed many of the barriers, particularly for poorer families, that had previously limited education for girls. A good education is also increasingly seen as an added qualification for marriage.

While men and women have equal rights under national, civil, and criminal law, men are sometimes preferred over women as employees, and tend to have a disproportionate representation in the most powerful decision-making positions. In civil disputes such as land inheritance, marriage, and divorce, many of the archaic personal laws still favor men. Even though the country was the first in the world to have a female prime minister and has also had a female president, women's political representation in Sri Lanka has historically been extremely poor, despite their forming half of the electorate. However, change is on the way. The February 2018 local government elections saw some 2,000 women elected to around 8,000 local government posts, as opposed to 82 in 2011. This was the direct result of an amendment passed in 2016 requiring 25 percent of political candidates to be women. Many of those elected campaigned on promises to end corruption and promote the rights of women and children, among them Rosy Senanayake, who was elected as Colombo's first female mayor.

Young girls in the household tend to assume their female roles from an early age, learning to adopt a demure demeanor in social situations. Sex before marriage is taboo—although in reality it happens in secret—and relations between men and women are generally formal, except between members of the extended family and long-term friends. Since women have more social responsibilities than men, girls are more strictly guarded than boys. In the cities—especially in Colombo—and among the more Westernized upper classes attending coeducational schools and colleges, girls and boys mix much more freely.

ATTITUDES TOWARD OTHERS

Sri Lankans have learned to live with plurality. Even during the civil war relations between ethnic groups were generally good away from the conflict zones. Physical differences between ethnicities are almost invisible—Tamils are believed to be darker-skinned than the Sinhalese, but this is often not the case—and usually the only barrier to relationships is language. All Sri Lankans have a similar core of cultural beliefs and values, especially in the fields of religion and family, and take great pride in their nationality. Intermarriage is becoming more common, and friends and families often share celebrations, cuisine, and religious festivals across the ethnic divide.

Since history has favored one or more ethnic group at one time or another, hostility and competition for political and economic power have periodically occurred in Sri Lanka. However, it should be remembered that the origins of the country's civil conflict were politically rather than socially motivated, being the result of a string of Sinhalese Buddhist-oriented policies of postindependence governments that marginalized the Tamil community. The LTTE was a Tamil militant organization, and only reflected the ideology of a small number of Tamils. While it is true that relations between the Sinhalese and the Tamils have been strained by years of civil war, Sri Lankans in general are keen to put this dark period behind them and show solidarity with one another.

Even so, there have been significant skirmishes in the postwar years between Sinhalese Buddhists and Muslims, a situation provoked by the actions of a Sinhalese Buddhist nationalist group of monks called the Bodu Bala Sena (BBS) which was formed in 2012 by the controversial figure Galagoda Aththe Gnanasara. Defining Sri Lanka as a purely Sinhalese Buddhist nation and not a multireligious country, the BBS campaigns against Christian and Muslim communities who are perceived to threaten Sinhalese Buddhist identity, often targeting businesses and inciting mob violence through hate speeches. Fatal riots in 2014 in Aluthgama and in 2018 in Ampara and Kandy, where Muslim businesses and homes were attacked, saw security forces slow to respond, and serve as examples of the country's enduring interethnic tension. BBS leader Gnanasara was subsequently jailed in 2018 for contempt of court and offensive behavior.

Attitudes Toward Foreigners

Sri Lankans enjoy meeting and conversing with foreigners, many of whom come to Sri Lanka on vacation. Warmhearted, talkative, and inquisitive, Sri Lankans often share food and drinks, and invite visitors home to meet their families and friends. While this is nearly always genuine, like anywhere in the world there are some who see foreigners as a possible gateway to material gain, and may want to make your acquaintance if they think there might be some advantage in it for themselves.

There are now many foreign expats living in Colombo and in the main tourist resorts, but less so in rural villages away from the coast. Whether in rural or urban areas, Sri Lankans will always warm to those who show genuine interest in and respect for their culture.

PRIDE AND "SAVING FACE"

The Sri Lankans are a proud people. They are proud of their history, their country, their achievements, and the robustness of their democratic institutions in the face of the myriad political and social challenges over the years. They are also especially proud of their cricket players, who are revered as royalty throughout the country. Sri Lankan Independence Day (February 4) has great significance, and is celebrated with pageants and parades of much pomp and ceremony.

As in most of Asia, emotional displays of any type are uncommon in public, where it is important to save "face" in social situations; on a Western level, this roughly translates as maintaining one's dignity in public. Face is much easier to lose than to keep, and it is of huge consequence to individuals when it is lost. Saving face is something Sri Lankans do to preserve not only their own dignity but also that of others; for example, by accepting assistance from someone even if help is not needed, or by taking care to lodge a complaint against a colleague in private rather than in front of his or her peers.

Sri Lankans will go to great lengths to avoid losing face, as this is seen as preferable to admitting they are unable or unwilling to do something. While this can be frustrating, since decisions are often avoided altogether for fear of failure, try to remember that it is done out of a natural desire to oblige. When Sri Lankans are asked a question to which the answer should be "no," many will give noncommittal, vague, or even positive answers to avoid disappointing the questioner or admitting that they cannot do something.

ATTITUDES TOWARD WORK

In general, Sri Lankans are hard workers who are honest in the workplace, dedicated to their job, and motivated by opportunities to improve their position. Many are entrepreneurs and dream of owning their own business.

Unemployment in Sri Lanka stands at around 4.7 percent, with the worst age bracket being those aged between fifteen and twenty-four years old (21.7 percent). Women often find it more difficult to find suitable jobs.

What appears to Westerners to be nepotism sometimes occurs in the Sri Lankan workplace, including in government, though it is mostly encountered in family businesses where younger family members may be promoted above others despite a lack of experience, education, or management skills. Relatives are seen as more loyal, and therefore more trustworthy. In larger businesses this practice is not so common, and while "help" might be given to members of their extended family by those in a position to do so, it would not be at the expense of others who have achieved their positions on merit.

ATTITUDES TOWARD TIME

Since the pace of life in Sri Lanka is slower than in the West, Sri Lankans are more relaxed when it comes to time. Schedules are often subject to delay, especially where public holidays and festivals intervene, congested roads disrupt journeys, and simple tasks take longer to accomplish. However, people have learned to take this into account by being realistic in most areas of their timekeeping and by leaving manageable gaps between appointments. A Sri Lankan may be ten to twenty minutes late for a meeting—rarely more—but this shouldn't prevent you from arriving on time. If you are meeting a Sri Lankan friend or colleague and realize that you are going to be late, it would be polite to give them a call to let them know.

PUBLIC DISPLAYS OF AFFECTION

Sri Lankans behave very conservatively in public. Although it is uncommon for couples, even when married, to kiss and hug openly when out and about, young couples are often seen in parks and seaview promenades huddled beneath umbrellas

in an (ironic) attempt to spend time together away from prying eyes. Members of the same sex often hold hands—especially young men—but this signifies friendship rather than sexual preference.

THE LGBT COMMUNITY

Homosexuality is illegal in Sri Lanka, despite being present in all levels of society and the efforts of a vocal gay community. While an attempt to decriminalize same-sex relationships was rejected by the cabinet in 2017, the government did at least commit to protecting the human rights of the LGBT community. Although no-one has ever been prosecuted for being homosexual, society is still bound by the negative connotations of homosexuality and LGBT people still face stigmatization and discrimination because of their sexual orientation, including in the workplace. As such, most LGBT people (especially those from low income families) keep this aspect of their lives secret from their families, and only open up to close friends.

chapter three

CUSTOMS & TRADITIONS

Festivals are an important part of daily life in Sri Lanka for every religion, bringing people together and strengthening relationships between family and friends. Many occasions, including rites of passage, are governed by auspicious times, hallowed by tradition and celebrated with festive food. Every major festival of each faith is represented in the public holiday calendar and, combined with every Buddhist full moon day (*poya*), means that there are at least twenty-five public holidays a year. While banks and offices are closed on public holidays, some shops and private enterprises may remain open, especially if the festival is not enjoined by the owner's faith; for example, a Muslim shop may continue to do business on a *poya* day.

POYA DAYS

Since ancient times Asian spiritual leaders have engaged in religious observances and refrained from worldly pursuits on full moon days. The Buddha later adopted this practice and when Buddhism was introduced to Sri Lanka *poya* days became part of the island's tradition. The Sinhalese word *poya* is derived from the Sanskrit *upavasam*, which, loosely, means a day of fasting and religious observance.

While each *poya* day, known by its traditional Sinhalese name, is related to an incident in the life of the Buddha, it also marks a (nonchronologically ordered) historic Buddhist event in Sri Lanka. The most important lunar month is Vesak (May), which is celebrated by Buddhists all over the world; Poson (June) comes a close second.

On *poya* days practicing Buddhists dress in white to visit the temple (*pansala*) and perform the rituals of worship, involving prayer, meditation, and listening to religious discourses. Ceremonies are conducted from dawn to dusk at all temples. The most devoted practitioners observe the eight precepts and, after noon, abstain from food and all forms of entertainment. Buddhist sermons and discussions are broadcast on national TV and radio.

The sale of alcohol and meat is strictly forbidden on *poya* days. Although you can eat meat in restaurants and hotels, you won't be able to purchase alcohol unless it's from your hotel mini bar. Beside their significance to Buddhists, *poya* days are also important for Hindus and, since each is a public holiday, those of other faiths may enjoy this observance by taking a day off work.

SRI LANKAN FESTIVALS

While Sri Lanka is predominantly a Buddhist country, its sizeable Hindu, Muslim, and Christian populations have resulted in it having one of the highest number of festivals a year in the world. Since most festivals follow the lunar calendar, where a full moon signifies the start of the lunar month, rather than the Gregorian calendar recognized by the West, some festival dates vary considerably from year to year.

Buddhist Festivals

Buddhist festivals typically revolve around *poya* days, of which there are typically twelve a year; one extra lunar month (*adhi*, meaning "half") is added every two or three years to keep the solar and lunar calendars aligned. Buddhist festivals are visual and colorful events that often involve weeks

of preparation. The biggest festivals are celebrated with *peraheras*—processions of dancers, drummers, singers, costumed elephants, and fire walkers—the largest and most famous of which is the ten-day Kandy Esala Perahera in July or August.

Hindu Festivals

Hindu festivals are numerous. Many are local, rather than national, and many take place in the temples of the Jaffna Peninsula. Characterized by color and

light, Hindu festivals are sometimes marked by the self-mortification of pious devotees as an act of faith or atonement. The most significant Hindu festival is held in Jaffna's Nallur Kovil over three weeks in August, while Kataragama's July/August festival comes a close second.

Muslim Festivals

Muslim festivals are observed by special prayers in the mosque followed by celebrations at home. They also follow the lunar calendar, but since extra months are not added the dates of these festivals move back at a rate of about eleven days a year. The most important Muslim festivals—Milad un-Nabi (the Prophet's birthday), Id ul-Fitr (the end of Ramadan), and Id ul-Allah (the beginning of the pilgrimage season to Mecca)—are all public holidays.

Christian Festivals

Although only a small proportion of the country is Christian, Western influence, especially in the cities and the tourist areas, has resulted in Christmas, for example, being noticeably celebrated in Sri Lanka. Artificial Christmas trees, cards, inflatable Santas, festive hats, and lights are sold at roadside stalls and in the bigger, highly decorated city malls weeks before the event itself. Passion plays are enacted in the island's Catholic communities during Easter, particularly in Negombo.

THE FESTIVE YEAR

January

Duruthu Poya commemorates the Buddha's first visit to Sri Lanka. The event is marked by a spectacular triple *perahera* at the Raja Maha Vihara temple in Kelaniya.

Thai Pongol is a Hindu festival held annually on January 14 and 15 that coincides with the end of the rice harvest. It is a two-day festival to thank the sun god Surya for his part in bestowing a successful yield. The first day is a public holiday (if it's not a weekend).

The Fairway Galle Literary Festival takes place every January (usually around the third weekend of the month), and welcomes eminent local and international writers, authors, poets, creatives, and visitors from around the world.

February

Navam Poya commemorates the Buddha's announcement of his impending death and nirvana. It is celebrated with a major *perahera* at the Gangaramaya Temple in Colombo.

Maha Sivarathri is held in February or March and is an important Hindu festival dedicated to Lord Siva. Pilgrims keep overnight vigils in temples by singing hymns, saying prayers, and fasting. It is a national holiday.

March

Medin Poya commemorates the Buddha's first visit to his parental home following his attaining enlightenment.

April

Bak Poya commemorates the Buddha's second visit to Sri Lanka.

Sri Lankan New Year falls on April 13 and 14. Known as Aluth Avurudhu in Sinhala, or Puththandu in Tamil, this is a nonreligious festival celebrated by Sinhalese and Tamils in their own unique way. The New Year signifies renewal, and houses are vigorously cleaned in preparation for the event; special food, especially sweet delicacies, are prepared; and presents, usually new clothes, are exchanged. Auspicious times signify the traditional carrying out of rituals and timings for the new year while fun games are organized in villages across the island. Visitors are often invited to join in. Businesses close for up to a week as many celebrants visit friends and family. It is a two-day public holiday.

Good Friday commemorates the death and resurrection of Jesus Christ. It is one of the most important Christian events in Sri Lanka, and many Catholic churches mark the occasion with passion plays and *peraheras*. It is an official public holiday.

May

Vesak Poya is for Buddhists the most important lunar month of the year, since it commemorates the triple anniversary of the Buddha's birth, enlightenment, and passing. It is especially significant for Sri Lankan Buddhists as it is when the Buddha paid his third and final visit to the island. This two-day festival and public holiday is marked by colorful illuminated handmade lanterns (*kudus*) displayed outside nearly every Buddhist home and business. Huge *pandols*—electronically lit platforms that display scenes from the life of the Buddha—are erected in towns, while food stalls (*dansalas*) distribute free food (rice and curry, ice cream, and the like) and soft drinks. White-clothed devotees flock to the temples to meditate, pray, and fast.

Republic Day or **National Heroes Day** on May 22 commemorates Ceylon's becoming the Republic of Sri Lanka in 1972, and honors all the Sri Lankan soldiers who died in the civil war.

June

Since it celebrates the introduction of Buddhism to Sri Lanka, **Poson Poya** is the second-most important Buddhist festival after Vesak. Devotees flock to Anuradhapura and Mihintale, the site where King Devanampiyatissa and his advisors were converted to Buddhism in 247 BCE.

July

Esala Poya commemorates the Buddha's first sermon since gaining enlightenment and also the arrival of the Buddha's Tooth Relic in Sri Lanka in the fourth century CE. While there are numerous nationwide celebrations in the month of Esala, including one at Kataragama, Kandy's world-famous ten-day pageant is the most spectacular and reflects the city's prestige in safeguarding the ancient tooth relic. Every night as many as a hundred bejeweled and illuminated elephants flanked by throngs of dancers, drummers, acrobats, and stilt walkers attract crowds in their thousands.

Usually held in either July or August, **Vel**, the most visual of Sri Lanka's Hindu festivals, is held in Colombo and commemorates the victory of Lord Murukan over the forces of evil. An ornate silver chariot bearing a statue of Murukan (or the war god Skanda) is born from Pettah to *kovils* in Wellawatta and Bambalapitiya, and is accompanied by scores of colorfully dressed pilgrims, dancers, musicians, and caparisoned elephants.

The **Kataragama Festival** in July/August is an occasion for pious devotees to fire-walk and perform acts of self-sacrifice to the Hindu god, Kataragama.

August

Nikini Poya marks the beginning of a three-month retreat (*vas*) for the monastic community.

Jaffna's **Nallur Festival** is a Hindu celebration in honor of the war god Skanda. Lasting twenty-five days, this is the island's longest festival. Huge chariot processions are enhanced by drumming and dancing while particularly enthusiastic devotees perform acts of self-mortification, such as driving silver spears or hooks through their bodies, in the belief that the gods will protect them from pain.

September

Binara Poya commemorates the Buddha's visit to heaven to preach to his mother and the celestial multitude.

The Hindu festival of **Dussehra** honors the supreme warrior goddess Durga. It also celebrates Rama's victory over the demon king Ravana in the legendary Indian epic *Ramayana*. Oil lamps are lit to invoke the blessings of Lakshmi, the Hindu goddess of wealth.

October

Vap Poya commemorates the conclusion of the Buddha's preaching in the heavenly realm and his return to earth, as well as the end of the monastic period of fasting.

Deepavali, or the Festival of Lights (Diwali) is a Hindu festival that falls in late October or early November and symbolizes the victory of good over evil. It is marked by the lighting of lamps and lanterns in Tamil homes and places of worship. It is a public holiday.

November

Il Poya commemorates the Buddha's ordination of sixty disciples to disperse his teachings.

December

Unduwap Poya commemorates the planting in Anuradhapura in 288 BCE of the sacred bo sapling brought from India by Emperor Asoka's daughter, Sangamitta, who also established the Bhikkhuni (Order of the Nuns). This sapling is said to have been taken from the historical bodhi tree under which the Buddha gained enlightenment in Bodhi Gaya, India, thought to be one of the oldest documented living trees in the world. Unduwap marks the start of the Adam's Peak pilgrimage season.

Christmas is celebrated by the island's Christian community and in tourist centers across the island on December 25th.

NATIONAL HOLIDAYS
February 4   Independence Day
May 1   Labor Day

CELEBRATING WITH FOOD

While Sri Lankan cuisine is renowned for being hot and spicy, the part it plays in celebrations is better known for its symbolism than for its flavor. For Buddhists and Hindus the sharing of food between family and close friends symbolizes the importance of reconciliation and harmony, while for Muslims, who often eat from the same plate, or *sahan* (which serves six persons), its importance lies in the equality of the community. Rice, a symbol of life and fertility, is the main food used in nearly every ceremonial occasion alongside more contemporary sweetmeats.

For Buddhists, most celebrations begin with the preparation of *kiribath* (rice cooked in coconut milk); it is a baby's first solid meal, it is the first food that the bride and groom share, and it is ritually prepared at the opening of a new business venture or when a couple moves into their new home, to ensure a lucky and propitious beginning. It is also the first meal eaten after the Sri Lankan New Year has dawned, often accompanied by *sambols* (spicy relishes prepared from onions, tomatoes, lime and chillis), *kokis* (deep-fried biscuits), and bananas.

For Hindus, *kiribath*, often boiled with *jaggery*—a coarse brown sugar made from the *kithul* palm—is also prepared for special occasions. At Thai Pongol all family members add a few morsels of rice to the boiling coconut milk to offer to the sun god in thanksgiving for the rice harvest. *Pongol* means "boiling over," and as the milk overflows it signifies abundance or prosperity. Buddhists perform a similar ritual at New Year and on other occasions that mark a new beginning.

Another traditional ritual performed by Buddhists at meal times is for the host to place a full glass of water on a tray and offer it to guests, who respond by lightly touching it. This act indicates that everyone present is invited to share in the occasion. The guests touch the glass to signify their appreciation at being invited to join in.

ASTROLOGY AND AUSPICIOUS TIMING

Astrology plays a significant role in the lives of nearly all Sri Lankans, Buddhists and Hindus, although it is a belief based on tradition rather than religion. Astrologers are highly regarded, and are nearly always consulted before Sri Lankans embark on any major enterprise in their personal, professional, or private lives, since they can foretell good or bad days according to a person's individual horoscope which is cast shortly after birth.

When Buddhist and Hindu children are born, the exact time, to the nearest minute, is recorded, as well as the date, so that an astrologer may use this information to cast a personal horoscope. This horoscope is then used by astrologers to help an individual move toward a prosperous life by suggesting good, appropriate, or auspicious times to commence tasks. If someone is venturing into a new business, for example, an astrologer will be consulted who will suggest an auspicious day and time for it to start, according to the horoscope of that individual. Rural people in particular have great faith in astrology, and it plays a dominant role in agriculture, especially in the cultivation of rice.

Auspicious times are used in rites of passage, such as in determining the best day and time for a baby to be fed its first solid meal, and are strongly adhered to when laying the foundation stones for new buildings and homes. For many aspects of marriage, such as the most auspicious times for the wedding date and the registration, both parties' horoscopes are considered. Astrology plays a significant role in cultural events, none more so than in the Sri Lankan New Year, when nearly every ritual is carried out at an auspicious time.

AYURVEDA AND HERBAL MEDICINE

The Ayurveda is an ancient Hindu system of medicine (from the Sanskrit *ayur*, life, and *veda*, knowledge) practiced in India and Sri Lanka that regards an illness as the result of an imbalance in a person's basic makeup. It seeks to cure disease by rectifying imbalances over time, through the examination of the whole of a patient's lifestyle, habits, diet, and emotional proclivities in order to find the root of the disease. Remedies come in a range of lotions, tablets, ointments, and oils, while therapeutic massages, healing wraps, and special diets are also commonly prescribed.

More than 75 percent of the Sri Lankan population believe that the ancient system of Ayurveda and the administration of herbal remedies are complementary to Western medical practices, and indeed they coexist happily side by side. For many, herbal medicines and Ayurvedic practitioners are also a cheaper alternative to visiting a Western doctor, and no less effective, since even conditions such as hypertension, rheumatism, and arthritis have been known to respond well to herbal treatments.

SUPERSTITIONS AND OMENS

Sri Lanka is a superstitious society. There is widespread belief in good or bad omens, such as whom you may meet at a particular time of the day, what they might say to you, or even what they might be carrying. Certain days of the week are considered ominous, animals are seen as omens of good or bad fortune, while death has numerous superstitions surrounding it.

AFTER A DEATH

- When brought to the funeral home, the body is always placed facing west.
- At least one person is present with the body at all times of the day or night, to prevent evil spirits from taking up residence in the house.
- Pictures are turned upside down so that the people in the photographs will not be possessed by the spirits of the dead.
- If a white cobra is encountered in a house, it is thought to be the spirit of the deceased relative who's returned to watch over the household.
- The body is always taken out of the funeral house feet first in order to disorient the spirit and prevent it from returning.
- The dead are usually not buried or cremated on a Friday or a *poya* day, as this is thought to have a devastating effect on the surviving family members.

Amulets, charms, and thread bracelets are worn by superstitious persons to ward off the Evil Eye. Newborn babies in Buddhist families wear the *Pancha-uda* (a gold or silver pendant embellished with five weapons—the bow and arrow, the conch, the sword, the trident, and the disc) until they are old enough to go to school. Hindus traditionally place a spot, or *potthu*, marked in red or black paste, on a baby's forehead to protect it from the Evil Eye. Sri Lankans rarely praise fortune on marriage, health, a relationship, or a pregnancy as some believe it will cause the opposite to occur.

When a person becomes ill, malicious spirits, or *yakkas*, are sometimes blamed, because they are believed to be capable of bringing about pathological states of the body and mind. Night-long healing ceremonies (*thovils*) are still commonly carried out in rural areas by exorcists (*kattadiyas*) to drive away these spirits through charms, offerings, and threats.

RITES OF PASSAGE

Each community has its own ceremonies for important occasions, such as birth, marriage, and death, which may be either social or religious in nature. According to each family's individual beliefs, desires, and financial means, these are celebrated either publicly or privately.

Birth and Early Childhood

Sri Lankans cherish children, so the birth of a baby, whether boy or girl, is a very important event. In the case of Buddhist and Hindu children, the exact time and date of the birth is recorded, and an astrologer is summoned to cast a horoscope, indicate an auspicious time for the child's naming ceremony, and give the first letter, or choice of letters, of the child's name.

According to Hindu tradition, soon after a birth the family goes through a period of ceremonial impurity for thirty-one days (although it can be shorter if there is an event already scheduled in the family), during which time they refrain from taking part in any religious ceremonies, including visiting the temple. After this a religious ceremony is performed and sandalwood paste is applied to the baby's newly shaved head after a bath. Also unique to Sri Lankan Hindus is the preparation of sweet *kolukattai*—crescent-shaped dough decorated with pieces of coconut to resemble teeth—to mark the occasion of the child's teething.

The Muslims have their own traditions. Since they do not believe in astrology, horoscopes are not cast. Instead, the first utterances a baby should hear are the *Azan*—the call to prayer—and the *Iqma*—marking the start of prayer. After seven days the baby's head is shaved and a name is chosen, which is customarily of Arabic origin.

A child's first solid food is typically *kiribath*, or a watered down rice soup, and the occasion is symbolically celebrated. Sinhalese families perform this custom six months or more after birth, after consulting an astrologer for an auspicious date and time for the occasion.

There is also an event to mark a child's advent into the world of learning. At the age of three or four, a ceremony is held whereby a teacher, priest, or learned elder in the family teaches the child to say and write the first letters of the Sinhalese or Tamil alphabet.

Coming of Age

A girl's coming of age (*kotahaluweema*) is celebrated after her first menstrual period, more commonly known as the occasion of her becoming a "big girl." While in past times this would have signified her availability on the marriage market, today it is an excuse for a party, where the traditional rituals are followed by gift giving and fun.

When a girl has her first period, she is customarily kept inside the house for about a week, seeing only her close family, not attending school, and eating only vegetarian food until the day of her ritual bathing as determined by an astrologer. The rituals start in the early morning, when the girl is bathed in holy water laced with jasmine flowers by an elder of the family and then dressed in new clothes and gold jewelry. The family then light oil lamps and share *kiribath* to mark her entrance into the adult world. Then the day is spent with the extended family and the party is held in the evening where invitees traditionally bring gifts of money and gold.

There is no specific rite of passage for boys.

Marriage Customs

Marriages in Sri Lanka are a sacred bond and a natural progression in a person's life. Arranged marriages still take place, especially among Hindu families; however "love matches," where young people choose their own partners, are now increasingly common. Caste is still a significant factor, while the matching of a couple's horoscopes—planetary compatibility—is of vital import, even among love matches. If the families of the young couple don't agree however, it is not uncommon for them to elope. The legal age for marriage is eighteen.

Once a marriage has been agreed on, Buddhists and Hindus consult an astrologer who sets a date for the wedding. The basic rituals and customs of each religion are thereafter adhered to while the extent of the celebrations varies according to the social and financial status of the families involved. If possible, couples will have two celebrations—a wedding and a homecoming—the latter being symbolic of the bride's arrival at her marital home. Alcohol will not be served at a Muslim wedding since it is forbidden under Islamic law.

A Buddhist wedding is a social union. Kandyan ceremonies are the most elaborate in dress and ritual. The main ceremony, which is centered on the beautifully decorated bridal platform (*poruwa*), is not religious, and is carried out by a master of ceremonies. The registration of the marriage may take place either before or after the *poruwa* ceremony, and is the only part that is legally binding. Some couples even register their marriage months in advance of the main event.

At the auspicious time, the bride and groom step on to the *poruwa* and the ceremony commences. Gifts, food, and betel leaves are given and exchanged between the couple and their families, while verses in Sinhala, Sanskrit, and Pali are read out to invoke the blessings of the deities. The most significant part of the ceremony is when the index fingers of the bride and groom are tied together with golden thread to symbolize the bond of marriage.

Hindu weddings are conducted by a priest and reflect the sacred union of the couple. They involve many symbolic rituals, including the giving by the

groom to the bride of a *thaali* (gold necklace) and *koorai* (sari) during the ceremony itself. The ceremony takes place around a fire, symbolizing Brahman, which the bride and groom must circle seven times to demonstrate their commitment and union.

A Muslim ceremony is both a social and a religious event, which typically consists of two parts: the *nikah*, or signing of the marriage contract in the mosque, and the consummation of the marriage. After the customary rituals have concluded, guests are treated to a lavish feast, called *waleema*. Celebrations may go on for days.

It is common for mixed-faith unions to marry with the customs of both religions.

Death

Each religious group observes its own customary funeral rites; Buddhists and Hindus prefer to cremate their dead, while Christians always bury theirs in order to facilitate their resurrection. Muslims also prefer to bury their dead, doing so without a coffin, within twenty-four hours of the death. Posters of the deceased are customarily pasted on to walls for all to see, while white flags strung along fences and roadsides provide a guided path to the funeral ceremony.

In most cases, except that of Muslims, the deceased lies in an open coffin in a "funeral house" (usually the family home of the deceased) for a set number of days, to allow friends and family to pay their respects. Oil candles are lit and windows are kept open for both superstitious and sanitary reasons. Food and drink is provided for the guests, many of whom pass the time chatting, playing carom, a popular local tabletop game, or cards.

When it is time for the funeral ceremony Hindu families surround the coffin, place oil on the deceased's head, and put rice and flowers inside the coffin. People wear light-colored clothing and often follow the coffin to the cemetery or burial ground on foot.

Most funerals are well-attended by the whole family and by those who knew the deceased or a member of their family; however Muslim and Hindu women (if it is a cremation) are not permitted to be present. Unlike in the West, funeral-goers generally favor white clothing.

After the funeral is over, families continue their vigil in the house, with the windows open, until seven days have passed. On the final day Buddhists offer *dana*, or alms, to monks. This practice—an offering whose merits it is hoped will be transferred to the dead—is performed again after three months, and yet again after a year to mark the first anniversary of the death, and annually from then on.

chapter four

MAKING
FRIENDS

Friendships in Sri Lanka tend to be forged at an early age. While the extended family is where most socializing takes place, people typically have a close circle of trusted friends from their school and village with whom they remain close throughout life, even if they don't see each other often. Loyalty and commitment are vital social obligations between friends, while patience, friendliness, courtesy, and restraint are highly valued virtues that instil both respect and confidence.

Very close friends are generally regarded in the same light as family, and within the circle they will do their utmost to help each other out when in need. While trust can take a long time to earn, especially if you are quite unknown (not only foreigners but also those from outside the family or social network), it can take seconds to lose, particularly if it involves pride or a loss of face. Wrongdoing between long-term friends is more easily forgiven.

Society is largely segregated by gender. Women, especially in more conservative rural areas, spend much of their time at home, while men are more likely to be out of the house, socializing in groups. Traditional social norms dictate that women and men, unless they are blood relations or close family friends, do not socialize freely before marriage. It is

therefore common for friendships outside the family circle to be between members of the same sex.

City dwellers and the Westernized upper classes in Colombo, however, socialize in a similar way to the West, and dating is common. Boys and girls mix freely in bars and clubs, go to parties and restaurants, and take weekend trips to the beach or the hills.

GREETINGS

While forms of greeting and methods of communication may vary between different ethnic groups, each possessing its own cultural nuances, the most important rules of social etiquette are universal. Forms of address, spatial distance, and intimacy typically mark differences in social rank. Eye contact is important, demonstrating interest and trust.

On formal occasions the Sinhalese traditionally greet each other by saying "*Ayubowan*," which means "May you be blessed with a long life." This word is accompanied by clasping the palms together, as if in prayer, close to the chest, and a slight bow or nod of the head, similar to the Indian *namaste*. It is considered polite to return the gesture. Tamils customarily greet people by saying "*Vanakkam*," which has a similar meaning, while Muslims might say "*Assalamu Alaikum*," the traditional Islamic greeting that means "Peace be upon you."

On a day to day basis, "Hello" is more common. In relaxed social settings, and especially among younger friends and acquaintants, Sri Lankans often say "*Kohomeda*?" ("How are you?") accompanied by a handshake, sometimes a head waggle, and often a broad smile. Close friends of the same sex, both male and female, may also give each other a quick hug or pat on the back and remain holding hands even after the initial handshake is over.

While handshakes, especially in business, are widely considered normal in modern-day Sri Lanka, some women may shy away from physical contact with unknown men, so it is polite for a man to shake a woman's hand only when she offers it. Since kissing is believed to be an intimate, and therefore private, form of affection, the "social" kiss, as a form of greeting, is less common. Family members may greet each other by touching cheek-to-cheek.

Sri Lankans address people respectfully, by using their appropriate title followed by their first name or surname. This is an acknowledgement of the status or seniority of that person. For this reason it is better to wait for the other party to move to first-name terms before you do. Sri Lankans often greet each other using nicknames or relationship terms such as *Mali*, which means younger brother, or *Nangi*, younger sister, or other titles such as *Mahattaya*, Sir, or *Nona*, Madam, in preference to using first names.

When greeting Buddhist monks, laypeople use a different form of address—"*Hamuduruwo*"—which is respectful and polite. They may also kneel down on the ground with head bowed as a mark of submission and respect. Children also perform this gesture as a mark of respect to their parents or elders. It is customary to bring ritual offerings of sacred betel leaves, areca nuts, and lime paste when visiting the Veddah community.

MEETING SRI LANKANS

When engaging a Sri Lankan in conversation don't be overenthusiastic. Be friendly, but also a little reserved, so that your sincerity is never in doubt. Making a good impression is vital, especially in business, when it might lead to an ongoing relationship. While eye contact is important in showing trust, remember that some Sri Lankans (such as Muslim women) might avoid this form of communication, either out of modesty or simply because they are shy— shy to speak English or because they might not be accustomed to meeting people from foreign cultures. The famous Sri Lankan smile often signifies welcome and warmth, but sometimes it covers embarrassment or confusion.

Sri Lanka is divided ethnically, politically, and by social status, so if you don't know someone well it is best to avoid controversial topics such as local politics. The best and safest topics to talk about are your family, your country, and what you do for a living. Sri Lankans are proud of their homeland, and your positive impressions of it will be very much appreciated. Similarly asking questions about their family will also make a good impression since the family unit is of the utmost importance in Sri Lankan society. Appearing genuinely interested is the key to success.

Sri Lankans have a good sense of humor, and are eager to use it. They are practical jokers, and enjoy teasing each other; but this is rarely intended to hurt the other person. Even when meeting someone for the first time there is no reason why you shouldn't use humor, but it will only be appreciated if it is well understood and universally accepted to be funny.

Directness is not common among Sri Lankans, who avoid the word "No" in case of causing disappointment. They also have a tendency to skirt around a point. Sometimes this means that disagreements between Sri Lankans that have been simmering below the surface will suddenly flare up, but anger, when aroused, is usually quickly diffused. Assertiveness is considered rude and aggressive.

With a little understanding, cultural gaps can be bridged through politeness and sensitivity. While you may never think exactly as a Sri Lankan does, you may come to a point when you can agree to disagree, with both parties making allowances for the other's different views. Since Sri Lankans are genuinely friendly, your chance meeting in a restaurant, on the beach, in a temple, or even on a train could turn into an invitation home, and from that into a lifelong friendship.

INVITATIONS HOME

Sri Lankans are very hospitable. If you have made some new Sri Lankan friends who want to get to know you better, or would like you to meet their families, they may well extend an invitation to their homes.

Bring them a present, but there is no hard and fast rule about what this should be. A dessert item such as ice cream is appreciated, as are chocolates, cookies, or fruit. Wrapped gifts are always put aside to be opened later. Flowers are associated more with funerals than weddings, and alcohol, such as a bottle of wine, should be given only if you know the family well. Women generally do not drink. Of course, you should not give alcohol if your hosts are Muslim.

In most households shoes should be removed before entering. If refreshments are offered it is impolite to refuse. If the invitation is for lunch or dinner, the menu is most likely to include rice, accompanied by an assortment of curries, sambols, and salads, as well as a dessert of fruit salad or ice cream. In Muslim homes a dinner of *buriyani* and roast chicken might be prepared for guests. Sri Lankans take great pleasure from their guests' enjoyment. Meals are expertly prepared in advance by the women of the household, and informally laid out on a table, buffet-style. In traditional homes the men often eat with the guests while the women, who pop in and out of the kitchen to refill curry bowls, eat later. Food may be spooned liberally onto your plate, so if you have had enough, a polite refusal accompanied by a compliment about the cooking will satisfy your hosts that you have enjoyed the meal. Water is typically offered after the meal, as well as perhaps soft drinks and tea, depending on the occasion and the time of day.

Sri Lankans eat rice and curry using their fingers, believing that this heightens the taste of the dish. If you want to do the same, your hosts will definitely approve. Use only the fingertips of your right hand to mix the rice and curries lightly into small bite-sized heaps to pop into your mouth. Avoid getting your palm and the rest of your fingers messy, as this is considered impolite. Wash your hands before and after eating. Most Sri Lankans, however, even those in rural villages, will recognize that foreigners do not all share this custom and will put out cutlery for their guests to use.

If you know a Sri Lankan Buddhist well, you may be invited for an almsgiving in their home—occasions when monks are invited to give a sermon for a deceased family member three months or a year after their passing. Alms in the form of food are given first to the monk and then to friends and family in order to bestow merit on the departed soul. Traditionally a rice and curry buffet is laid out on mats on the floor for everyone to help themselves. It is customary to bring a simple gift of sugar, milk powder, or cookies.

When their guests are leaving, Sri Lankans will wave good-bye from their doorstep until they are completely out of view.

DRESS
Both traditional and Western styles of dress are common in Sri Lanka. Sri Lankans take pride in their appearance and very much appreciate others

who do so too. Women, especially in rural areas, cover up much more than those in the Western world, typically wearing long dresses and skirts, and shirts with sleeves when they are out of their homes, though jeans are common among the younger generation.

While the men jump around on the beach often wearing nothing more than their underwear, women swim fully clothed. Western women are not expected to do the same, and bikinis are a common sight in tourist resorts, as are skimpy tops, short skirts, and shorts. Such clothing may be acceptable wear for the beach, but when in towns and visiting temples and people's homes modest dress should be worn out of respect for the local culture. The more revealing a woman's clothing, the more unwanted attention she will receive from Sri Lankan men, who may mistake her taste in clothes for promiscuity.

Weddings and other important social functions are occasions to look one's best. Saris are still the preferred formal dress of women, but today have many modern variations. Westernized outfits such as dresses and high heels are gaining in popularity with the younger generation. Men wear suits or smart trousers, shirts, and ties for formal occasions.

chapter five

AT HOME

Sri Lanka is traditionally an agrarian society, and more than three-quarters of the population still live in rural areas. Those who have migrated to the cities in search of employment retain close ties with their villages through their family and land ownership.

Housing varies greatly according to socioeconomic status and location. In poorer rural areas people may live in very simple wattle and daub structures with mud floors and thatched roofs, while urban Sri Lankans might live in high-rise apartments,

refurbished heritage homes, and condos. A great many buildings remain from the colonial era, and many of these are highly sought after and have been beautifully restored.

A typical Sri Lankan house is characterized by whitewashed (or sometimes candy-colored) walls, red polished cement floors, and windows with built-in vents to allow for the circulation of air. Roofs are tiled or made of corrugated asbestos. Houses have one to four rooms, a central living area, and a kitchen and laundry room generally located at the back. Outhouse bathrooms with squat toilets are still common in rural areas. Front and back verandas typically open onto a garden or yard filled with colorful potted plants and fruit trees.

The interior tends to be very simple. Plastic chairs and tables are common and are a cheaper alternative to wood, while curtains are used instead of interior timber doors. The pictures on the walls are usually family photos, a calendar, and a religious image placed above a small shrine, where residents light candles and incense and say prayers. A vase of plastic flowers may provide color. Many homes now have televisions and satellite connections are becoming more widespread.

Electricity in Sri Lanka is very expensive for most people and is provided by the government-run Ceylon Electricity Board. The high cost of air conditioning means most homes rely on fans to keep them cool. Power cuts are frustratingly common, especially in rural areas, and the rate per unit increases the more you use.

THE HOUSEHOLD AND EXTENDED FAMILY

Among all ethnic groups in Sri Lanka, both the nuclear and the extended family are vital social units. The extended family is an important social network that provides support to the nuclear family—even newlyweds are rarely alone for long, as relatives come and go, and sometimes stay for long periods of time, especially if help is needed with young children. Large family reunions are held during traditional festivals such as Sri Lankan New Year.

Families are more scattered than they used to be, and an increasing number of newlyweds live in their own homes if they can afford it. However, there is still a preference for living close to, or even with, their parents or in-laws. Wives typically enjoy good relationships with their own family, relying on their mother for support when their children are born.

Sri Lankans traditionally have a deep respect for their elders, and parents live with their children once they are unable to support themselves. It is uncommon for anyone to live alone.

The traditional head of the household is the husband, and in his absence the eldest son assumes this role. However, nearly a quarter of Sri Lankan households today are headed by women in the absence of a suitable man; the tsunami, the past civil conflict, and migration to work abroad (though many women also migrate to work overseas) are the main contributory factors to this situation.

Although the roles of the sexes in the household are clearly defined, in many cases there is a good deal of equality between spouses. Women are traditionally responsible for housework, cooking, and raising the children, as well as taking care of the family finances, while the men provide economic stability and represent the family in their public affairs. In agricultural families, women are in charge of weeding and harvesting the crops, while men do the plowing, sowing, and threshing.

Increasingly, husband and wife together make important family decisions, such as the choice of suitable marriage partners for their children. The children traditionally see their father as the role model, while from their mother comes emotional stability and spiritual growth. In urban areas, the frequency of women working has resulted in men becoming more actively involved in the emotional and practical day-to-day aspects of child rearing.

RESPECT FOR ELDERS

Sri Lanka's elderly population is one of the fastest growing in Asia. As we have seen, socially and culturally, Sri Lankans have a deep respect for the elderly, both in the home and in public life. Older people are respected as valuable resources with vital skills, experience, and wisdom from which the younger generation is able to benefit when seeking advice and counsel. They are involved in family-based rituals and are the custodians and transmitters of cultural traditions.

Religion has also encouraged the social care of the elderly, and in old age parents typically live with their children. Institutional old-age homes do exist in Sri Lanka, but they are not nearly as numerous as in the Western world and are often small and underfunded. Even in the most unavoidable circumstances, when the family is financially unable to look after an elder, or when they are simply unwilling to do so, an institution is largely seen as a socially unacceptable choice.

THE DAILY ROUTINE
Life in the Village
Rural village life revolves mainly around agriculture. Women generally wake up early to make breakfast for the family, get the children ready for school, and do the household chores. The men go to work in the fields and come home for lunch, which is the main meal of the day. Families usually eat their evening meal together. In many rural households the women also do other work, fitting this around their household duties. The extended family helps with child care.

The pace of life in the village is slow, picking up at harvest time, when there is a great deal of hard work to be done. Settlements are characterized by a place of worship, and religion plays an important role

in the daily life of the population. At home, many
people light incense and oil candles each morning,
and offer prayers to their small Buddhist or Hindu
shrines.

Houses in many rural settlements do not have
a bathroom but only a simple outside squat toilet.
Most water has to be drawn from wells, and where
people don't have a well of their own they go to a
communal well or tank, or a stream or river, to fetch
water and wash. The mornings and evenings are
typically when men go to bathe, before and after
work, and the middle of the day is generally the time
for women and children, who take their laundry and
cooking utensils along to wash at the same time.

Mornings in the villages are full of sound, as
mobile vendors selling anything from fresh fish to
curd melodiously cry their wares, and the ice cream
and bread vans play their own special tunes. Rural
Sri Lankans prefer to shop for fresh food at their
weekly village market (*pola*) where seasonal fruit,
vegetables, meat, and fish, and other items such as

clay cooking pots and plastic tableware, can all be purchased relatively cheaply.

Sri Lanka's Tamil plantation workers are among the island's most disadvantaged and isolated groups. In the plantations, the workers typically live on the estates with their families in "line houses" (small adjoining units) located close to the tea fields. Overcrowding is common. Since estate owners are also responsible for providing their workers with social services such as housing, water, and health care, residents are highly dependent upon them. Schools are often understaffed, and children have few role models outside the plantation industry to gain knowledge of other possible occupations. While many children leave school early to help their families on the estates, increasing numbers are opting to further their education and seek out jobs in cities and towns.

Life in the Town

The migration of rural Sri Lankans to the cities is increasingly common. While many leave for urban centers such as Colombo to search for better occupations, many also circulate around the country as a result of the growing tourism industry. Shelter can be an issue for unsupported migrants—some of whom are two or three generations away from their rural roots—who might live in slums and shantytowns located on marginal lands such as canal banks and railway reservations. New modern housing developments and high-rise condominiums (nearly all of them private) are popping up everywhere, particularly in Colombo's city center, yet also along the south and west coasts. Renting a home is common though in cities the rates can be very high.

Urban centers such as Colombo demonstrate that modern Sri Lanka is a fusion of old and new. Huge mansions in gated compounds patrolled by security guards sit next to poorly built *watte*—wooden planked houses with roofs made from corrugated metal sheets; modern skyscrapers and condominiums overlook canal-side shantytowns; and upscale shopping malls stand beside rustic tea shops.

While the majority of city people rely on overcrowded buses and trains to get to work, as well as motorbikes, tuk-tuks, and taxis, an increasing number of Sri Lankans have their own cars and perhaps even a personal driver. All, however, have to contend with severe traffic congestion and delays, and the resulting pollution.

City dwellers prefer the convenience of shopping in large, air-conditioned supermarkets, networks of which are now found in nearly all towns across the island; however all urban areas also have defined market areas.

After work, younger urbanites socialize in restaurants, bars, and clubs, or in parks and shopping malls, and on weekends and bank holidays take the opportunity to get away from the city and head for the hills or coast.

GROWING UP IN SRI LANKA

In Sri Lanka children are cherished, adored, and indulged. Babies are carried until they can walk, and small children are traditionally kept with their mothers until they are old enough to go to school around the age of five. Babysitting is uncommon and unnecessary since the extended family provides extensive support. Affluent families and foreign expats often have domestic servants and live-in nannies to

provide them with child care, taking them with them on trips and vacations if necessary. You won't find child care facilities in restaurants or workplaces and, except for in high-end hotel chains, creches and indoor play areas are rare. Most towns and cities do have parks with swings

and slides, however, though these are often very basic metal installations. Once the children are past their early years, both parents share in their upbringing and discipline.

Sri Lankan children learn modesty, self-control, obedience to their parents, and loyalty to their family. Girls and boys mix freely until puberty, and in their teens begin to adopt their adult roles. Girls help with the household chores and learn domestic skills such as cooking, while boys have more freedom to explore their surroundings.

In urban areas and among the Westernized elite boys and girls mix much more freely in their spare time, going shopping and visiting cafés and each other's homes, or going to sports and other clubs.

TV AND THE TELEDRAMA

Most Sri Lankan households now have a television, and cable connections are increasingly common. A range of local networks broadcast a variety of programs, from news and political satires to children's cartoons and films; while those with satellite connections have access to a vast array of channels including movies, TV shows, news and sports. In rural villages, where fewer households have television sets, people crowd the doorways and verandas of their neighbors' houses to watch Sri Lankan cricket matches, news programs, cultural shows, religious programs, and political satires. The ubiquitous "teledrama" (soaps), both local and Hindi, broadcast every evening, are favorites across all levels of society.

chapter **six**

TIME OUT

Sri Lankans love their time out but don't generally go on vacations in the Western sense of the word. Difficulties in getting visas for foreign travel for Sri Lankan passport holders (and the expense of foreign travel) mean that most holiday at home. Any free time, such as on the occasion of a major religious or cultural event, is taken as an opportunity to go as a group to visit extended family and friends, or with them to attend a family occasion. Vans and buses are hired as they head for the beaches or hills, temples or pilgrimage sites, historical attractions or wildlife parks, the sound of song and drums typically indicating their arrival long before they come into view.

Sri Lankans will find a way to enjoy themselves wherever they go. In groups they demonstrate a much greater confidence and a more outgoing personality than they do as individuals. Most working adults, especially those living away from home, cherish the occasions when they are able to spend time off with family and friends.

There is plenty to see and do in Sri Lanka, much of it outdoors. The country has an abundance of beaches, wildlife parks, rain forests, historic cities, and archaeological sites, as well as many fascinating religious buildings. While few Sri Lankans go trekking or cycling (though they do love going on safari in the island's national parks), a number of tour companies offer fascinating trails, which are a perfect way for the visitor to get off the beaten path and experience authentic Sri Lankan life. Visiting one of the many cultural, historical, and religious attractions at festival times may be crowded and noisy, but is a great way to meet people and immerse oneself in Sri Lankan culture.

SRI LANKANS ON TOUR

When going on a pilgrimage or visiting a temple, Buddhists and Hindus put coconut palm flowers on the front of their vehicles, while for protection and luck a pendant of lime and chili is attached to the bumper. The town of Kataragama—a pilgrimage site for Buddhists, Hindus, and Muslims—and Adam's Peak, or Sri Pada—a holy site for these three·faiths and for Christians as well—are the two most sacred and popularly visited pilgrimage spots.

Family days out are more common than weeklong stays, while long weekends at the beaches or in the hills are much enjoyed by groups of male friends and the mixed Colombo crowd. Structured group tours, predominantly within Sri Lanka but also to India and Thailand, are organized by local temples for a reasonably priced package that includes transportation by bus and accommodation—most often in temples. Having an itinerary that takes in the major religious and cultural attractions, these trips most closely resemble a Western-style package tour, and are popular one-off events for Sri Lankans who can afford it.

Since Sri Lankans much prefer the taste—and economies—of home cooking, all of the necessary culinary equipment, including gas stoves, is usually taken with them on their tour. Whether staying with family or in a local guesthouse, the women will set up their own cooking place in the morning to make breakfast for the family and then prepare lunch, which is packed into tiffin carriers (metal lunch boxes) and plastic boxes to be eaten at an attractive stopping point in the journey—often beside a river, a lake, or the sea, to facilitate washing as well as combine with a swim. Many also frequent local roadside *kades* (simple restaurants), which serve breakfast, lunchtime rice and curry and evening *rotis* (local flatbreads), hoppers (crispy bowl-shaped pancakes), and *kothu,* a dish of chopped *roti*, vegetables, sometimes chicken, and curry sauce that's cooked on a hot plate.

TEMPLE ETIQUETTE
While most devout Buddhists will visit their local temple on *poya* days, and take with them offerings of flowers, food, and oil candles, devotees of Buddhism and Hinduism may travel to other important temples

or *devales* (shrines to particular Hindu gods) further afield to offer worship and say special prayers. The town of Kataragama is the most popular place of veneration. Devotees travel long distances to this sacred place, since it is believed that wishes made and prayers said here have a much higher chance of being answered. Buddhist temples and Hindu *kovils* welcome respectful visitors, but mosques do not.

Nearly every Buddhist temple has a *dagoba* (white domed structure), a sacred bodhi tree, a Buddha statue, and an image house, where devotees make offerings. The tree is significant, as it was under a bodhi tree that the Buddha gained enlightenment. Devotees light oil lamps, offer flowers (the blooming of a flower upon contact with light is seen as symbolic of the attainment of enlightenment), and circle the tree or *dagoba* three times in a clockwise direction. Wishes are written on scraps of material, folded with a coin, and colorfully tied onto the boughs of the bodhi tree in the hope that the wish will come true.

When visiting a temple it is important to keep the impact of your presence to a minimum. Buddha images are considered as sacred as the Buddha himself and, along with monks, are respected accordingly. You should never be photographed with your back to a Buddha nor take photos of monks without permission. Buddhist priests have a special place in Buddhist society, being the third of the three elements of veneration—the Buddha (teacher), the Dhamma (teachings), and the Sangha (order of monks).

Visitors, both men and women, should dress modestly at religious sites, covering shoulders and legs. Hats and sunglasses should be removed. When Buddhist and Hindu devotees come to the temple for worship they ritually bathe and then dress in fresh, clean, light-colored clothes. Shoes should always be removed when entering any temple grounds, even a ruined one, as this is considered no less sacred.

SHOPPING FOR PLEASURE

Most shopping is done in independent retail outlets rather than markets (except for the village *pola*). Sri Lanka is famous for its garment exports, and internationally branded goods can be found at relatively cheap prices. Locally handcrafted items include wooden carvings, baskets, hand-loom textiles, brasses, and silverware.

Western-style department stores and air-conditioned malls are predominantly found in Colombo though they also exist in large urban centers such as Kandy and Galle. Some have food courts, which are frequently populated with groups of young people, shoppers, and office workers taking a break for lunch.

In most stores you have to leave your shopping bags in monitored cubbyholes at the entrance. The security guard gives you a tag, which you exchange for your things when you leave.

Sri Lanka can be one of the best places in the world to buy reasonably priced gems, but beware of con artists trying to pass off colored glass. Purchasing from street vendors is a high-risk gamble, and it is best to buy from a government certified store, where guarantees are provided upon purchase. The Sri Lanka Gem and Jewellery Exchange in Colombo will test gems free of charge.

Credit cards are accepted in all major stores and supermarkets, although in some of the smaller shops you may have to pay some commission. For street and market shopping it is best to have cash in small denominations, especially if you are bargaining. Be aware of tour guides or tuk-tuk drivers pressing you to visit particular shops, as their commission will inflate the final price.

Sri Lankan New Year is the most frenzied shopping time, with shoppers hunting for bargains weeks in advance of the big day. The most commonly given presents are clothes, and many street vendors set up special stores for the event and offer tempting discounts as the New Year approaches.

Bargaining

While prices in independent retail shops are fixed, bargaining at street stalls, markets, and casual tourist shops is common. Foreigners are often expected to pay a "tourist price" that is much higher than the sum the locals pay. If you are looking for something in particular, do a little research first, and in agreeing on a fair price consider the time and effort that have gone into making the item. Retain a sense of humor and proportion: a small saving for you can be a significant amount to the seller.

CULTURAL ACTIVITIES
Music

Sri Lankan music has been influenced by religious chanting, the rhythm of African slave songs, and the melodies, charisma, and commercialization of South Indian (Bollywood) culture. Drums have been an integral part of Sri Lankan music for centuries, and remain the main rhythm setter today. Other classical

Sri Lankan instruments include the *thalampata* (two small cymbals on a string), the reed flute, and the *hakgediya*, or conch shell, which is used to open ceremonies.

The Portuguese and British colonizers brought African slaves (known as *kaffirs,* the Arabic word for "unbelievers") to the island, who introduced a style of music commonly known as the *baila*, characterized by an increasingly frantic, bouncing rhythm. While Western music, especially dance music, is growing in popularity among young Sri Lankans, *baila* is still the favorite form of pop music throughout Sri Lanka, and is heard in homes, on buses, and at weddings and parties.

Dance

Sinhalese legend dictates that Sri Lanka's classical dancing originated 2,500 years ago, when a magical dance ritual broke a spell on a bewitched king. Dance is an integral part of the Sri Lankan culture, and is performed on every festive occasion. It is always accompanied by the rhythmic beat of drums, cymbals, and bells. The most prominent styles are the Kandyan (*uda rata natum*) and masked, or low-country (*pahatha rata natum*), dances. Each style differs in the costume, the method of body movement, and rhythm (*tala*), as well as the type of drum used.

Out of the five types of Kandyan dancing, it is the sacred *ves* dance that is most commonly seen at festivals and *peraheras* throughout the island. The *geta bera*, or double-ended drum, typically provides a frenzied beat that encourages the elaborately dressed dancers to leap and flip energetically into the air.

The *yak bera* drum is used in low-country dances such as *kolam* (see Theater, below) and *sunni yakuma* (healing dance ceremony, or devil dance), which both feature elaborately carved masks. These dances often reflect the ancient folk belief-system of Sri Lanka's pre-Buddhist agricultural civilization, when a variety of demons and deities were thought to cause afflictions and diseases. Masks representing the various demons are worn to appease them or scare them away.

Cinema

Not surprisingly, Sri Lanka's cinematic style is
similar to that of India, since it has been influenced
by Bollywood. Released in 1956, *Rekawa* ("Line of
Destiny"), the first feature film by the internationally
renowned Sri Lankan director Lester James Peiris,
was the first movie to be shot entirely in Sri Lanka.
Like Hindi movies, Sri Lankan ones are often love
stories set in rural villages or across ethnic divides,
and many relate to the civil war.

Sri Lanka has a modest number of cinemas in the
major towns and cities, and some of these have 3D
screens. Halfway through is an interval, when soft
drinks, snacks, and ice creams are sold. Sri Lankan,
Hindi, and Hollywood movies are also shown on
television and these, along with popular TV series
from around the world, are widely available to rent or
buy from shops selling mostly pirated DVDs. When
a new movie comes out, whether in Sinhala, Tamil,
or Hindi, huge billboards announce its arrival, and
Tamil or Sinhalese subtitles make it accessible to all.

Theater

Theater in Sri Lanka has its origins in the traditional
rituals, customs, and folk drama of the nineteenth
century. Villagers would get together and act out
masked dances (*kolam*) and satirical sketches using
familiar characters such as the king, town clerk,
policeman, and the farmer and his wife, as well as
gods, demons, and animals. By the mid-twentieth
century, this ritualistic form of dance drama
amalgamated with influential Western theater
methods to create a new style of modern theater
in Sri Lanka.

Plays and comedies by Shakespeare and other famous playwrights, along with popular musicals and the odd international production, are sporadically staged in schools, community centers, and theaters such as the Lionel Wendt. Complex, thought-provoking, and often controversial Lanka-centric productions by talented young writers and directors are also staged a few times a year.

Village communities host their own plays on special occasions, while Christians stage passion plays at Easter. Performed within the Indian Tamil communities of the Hill Country in May, the *Kamenkoothu*—an ancient folk drama telling the story of the Hindu god of love—unites whole villages and lasts for several days.

SPORTS

Sri Lankans have a positive attitude toward sports, and enjoy both playing and watching them. While volleyball is the official national sport, cricket is by far the most popular. Sri Lanka's cricket team gained Test status in 1982 and quickly became one of the best in the world, especially in one-day matches. In 1996 Sri Lanka won the Cricket World Cup. They were runners up in 2007, and in 2011 when they were one of the host countries, though they failed to reach the final in 2015.

Evidence of Sri Lanka's love for cricket is everywhere. Children and teens play games on any available patch of land, using whatever they can find in the way of bat and ball. When important international matches are televised fans crowd around every available television and radio set to cheer on their team. Live matches, in one of the many good stadiums island-wide, are characterized by a vocal crowd and a vibrant, carnival-like atmosphere, and tickets are still fairly cheap. Former players such as the wicket-keeping all-rounder Kumar Sangakara and record-breaking spin bowler Muttiah Muralitharan (Murali) are considered national heroes.

Other popular sports in Sri Lanka are football, swimming, netball, badminton, and athletics. Played in the more famous educational establishments in Colombo, Kandy, and Galle, rugby union also has quite a following. The Dialog Colombo Sevens is an annual rugby tournament contested in Colombo by teams from eight Asian nations.

Sri Lanka has its own version of baseball called *elle* (pronounced el-lay). While the gist of the game is similar, in *elle* the ball is smaller and the bat is replaced by a long bamboo stick. *Elle* is played in schools and in communities at festive periods, especially Sri Lankan New Year.

EATING OUT
Sri Lankan Cuisine

Sri Lankan cuisine is fierier than that of its Indian neighbor. Fresh chilies or chili powder are liberally added to most curries—generally, the darker or redder the gravy, the more intense the heat. Rice is the main

staple and is eaten in one form or another at all meals; string hoppers (steamed vermicelli-like nests), plain hoppers (crispy bowl-shaped pancakes), and *pittu* are all made from rice flour. Fiery *sambols* of coconut, tomato, onion, chili, and dried Maldive fish typically act as flavor enhancers. Most curries are cooked in oil (coconut or vegetable) and may contain coconut milk, but Sri Lankan food is relatively healthy, and the wide variety of pulses, lentils, and fresh vegetables used make it an ideal cuisine for vegetarians.

Sri Lanka has an abundance of tropical fruits, and so it is not surprising that the most common dessert—or breakfast—is either a fruit platter or a deliciously sweet fruit salad. Fresh juices are available everywhere, as is king coconut water, alongside soft drinks and bottled water. Buffalo curd is blended into the drink *lassi,* or served with rich *kithul* palm honey as a traditional dessert.

Restaurants

There is a wide variety of eating establishments, ranging from the most basic rice and curry *kades* (shops) and bakeries serving "short eats" (buns, pastries, and *roti* bread) found everywhere, to air-conditioned restaurants serving international cuisine in Colombo and top hotels island-wide. Independent restaurants are abundant in towns and tourist resorts, where the menus will feature a large selection of Eastern and Western dishes including plenty of fish, seafood, and sometimes beef and pork. Fish fresh from the Indian Ocean is preferred over the softer, less tasty river fish. Muslim establishments only sell *halal* meat and never pork. Remember the dietary rules when ordering, or when picking a restaurant in which to meet a Muslim friend.

Kades sell Sri Lankan food and rarely have a menu; expect rice and curry for lunch, hoppers and *sambol* for dinner, and sweet Ceylon tea. Tea is served at any time of the day with or without milk and normally with lots of sugar unless you request otherwise. While Sri Lankans traditionally eat with their fingers, cutlery is always available if you ask. Rice and curry in local *kades* can often be far better and much more authentic than you would find in a five-star hotel. Those located on main thoroughfares see a large quantity of customers on a daily basis, which ensures that the food is very fresh. Don't be put off by the gloomy, messy appearance of some *kades*, as most are quick, tasty, clean, and very good value.

Smarter than *kades* are "hotels," which are also found across the island. Rather than places to stay, these are actually local restaurants that are well patronized by travelers, office workers, and commuters. Most menus feature a range of dishes such as fried rice, noodles, *chop suey* (a Chinese dish), and deviled meats. While in many cases the food is good, Sri Lankans will still agree that it is not comparable with what they get at home!

Cafés, coffee shops, and restaurants serving international dishes and nutritious world cuisine are common in Colombo, and in south and west coast tourist centers. Many offer innovative fusion Sri Lankan–Western menus at fair prices, and an atmosphere that is casual, convivial, and relaxed.

Fast-food chains are found in the cities, and most offer home delivery. Food courts with a selection of world cuisine are found in some of the city's larger shopping malls and are well patronized throughout the day. Lunch packets are probably the island's cheapest and most well-known take-out option: a portion of rice and a variety of curries are wrapped up in plastic sheets, parceled up in newspaper, and sold in *kades* or on the street.

If you have invited Sri Lankan friends out for dinner, it is customary for you to pay the bill. If they have invited you, it is polite for you to offer to pay, though you may be refused. If you are hosted for dinner in a restaurant, it is polite to return the invitation at some point in the near future.

TIPPING

Tipping is expected in Sri Lanka, since wages are low. While most restaurants and some hotels include a 10 percent service charge on the bill, Sri Lankans might also leave a further 10 percent tip on top of this. Tipping is a way of showing your appreciation and understanding of the realities of life for the workers. Wealthier Sri Lankans may tip more frequently—to a shop assistant who carries their bags to their car; to someone who finds and saves them a seat on a busy bus or train; and to a doorman who runs an errand for them. It is customary to tip housekeepers and bellboys, and taxi or three-wheeler drivers if they have given you good service. Stick to small tips rather than large sums of money.

NIGHTLIFE

Nightlife is increasingly varied in the cities, and offers something for everyone. There are restaurants and bars in every town, but since only the most Westernized women drink, local bars outside Colombo and the tourist areas tend to be dingy and male-oriented. Many men prefer to buy alcohol more cheaply in a liquor store and drink somewhere else with their friends.

The southwestern coastal areas cater to the tourist trade through casual beach bars and seasonal discos. In Colombo, pubs, bars, and clubs offer Western-style entertainment, including live bands, big-screen international sports fixtures, and karaoke, as well as an increasing range of gourmet restaurants. There are also some casinos. Across the rest of the island, nightlife is generally more low key and restaurant-focused. Party planners and DJs arrange frequent glitzy club nights in hotels, sports grounds, and beach resorts in or outside the city, often inviting visiting international artists, and these are well attended by the Colombo crowd.

Imported spirits are widely available in the larger hotels and restaurants, but they are expensive. Wine too is comparatively costly, though the selection has got better in recent years, especially in the top end hotels and restaurants. Most Sri Lankans drink the national beverage, *arrack*—distilled from the sap of coconut palm flowers—or stick to local vodka, gin, and rum, while those with more money may have a penchant for whiskey too. Beer has been produced locally since the nineteenth century, and remains popular. The local brand is Lion and is most commonly sold in reusable bottles that hold 625 ml (just over one and a third pints) or cans.

chapter seven

TRAVEL, HEALTH, & SAFETY

With a wealth of beautiful beaches, archaeological attractions, tea-clad hills, and national parks filled with wildlife, Sri Lanka is an incredibly diverse travel destination. While there are many forms of transportation available, long journeys on congested and often poorly surfaced roads do require patience. Travelers should be very aware of road etiquette, whether they are driving, cycling, or on foot.

Travel in Sri Lanka is a multisensory experience of sound and spectacle. Buses and trains are often overcrowded, so expect impromptu musical performances, food vendors, delays, and sweaty journeys with lots of social interaction. Taxis allow for relative peace and privacy.

Compared with much of Asia, the standards of hygiene in Sri Lanka are reasonable, and the country has a good health care system. It is also one of the better places in the region for women to travel alone, provided they act responsibly and take sensible precautions.

ROADS AND TRAFFIC
Driving
While most foreign visitors to Sri Lanka opt to hire a car and driver rather than self-drive, those wishing

to drive themselves need to be confident and assertive. To drive in Sri Lanka you need to get your existing driver's license or International Driving License (known as IDP) verified by the Department of Motor Vehicles or the Automobile Association (AA) in Colombo. To obtain a full Sri Lankan license your Sri Lankan visa will need to be valid for six months or more. Driving is on the left and the minimum driving age is eighteen.

Traveling by road can be a frustrating experience. Despite Sri Lanka's modest size, roads are often congested with cars, lorries, buses, tuk-tuks, motorbikes, bicycles, and even wildlife, so expect extended journey times. There is an average speed of 35 kmph (22 mph) in the hills, and 55 kmph (34 mph) on main roads. Google maps has Sri Lanka covered and these days is fairly accurate in calculating journey times.

Sri Lanka now has a handful of speedy expressways (known locally as highways) or toll roads, and a couple more under construction. The first to open in 2011 was the Southern Expressway, which links Colombo with Galle and Matara, and is expected to reach Hambantota by the end of 2019. Other expressways include the Colombo–Katanayake Expressway (for the international airport) and the Outer Circular Expressway, which is basically just a northern extension of the Southern Expressway though it doesn't yet reach Katanayake. The speed limit on expressways is 100 kmph (which is rigidly controlled by speed camera-wielding policemen) and tolls vary between LKR100 and LKR450.

For the foreign visitor the experience of driving, or even being driven, on Sri Lanka's chaotic roads can be alarming. Urban centers and busily congested highways, where the more forceful vehicles such as buses and trucks assert their domineering might over softer road users such as motorcycles, bicycles, and bullock carts, are not for the fainthearted. However, despite the chaos there is a method to this madness, and a large amount of the weaving, light flashing, and honking is an organized art form that new drivers will soon get to learn. The key is to always allow plenty of time to travel, and never drive (or be driven) anywhere in a hurry.

While there are rules for driving in Sri Lanka, most are disregarded and few are ever enforced, expressway speed limits excluded. Instead Sri Lankans follow a secret highway code that gives the biggest vehicles supreme right of way as buses aggressively tailgate and honk at anything smaller in their path. Vehicles will demand right of way by flashing their headlights. Sri Lankan drivers are some of the most horn-happy in the world, and the use of the horn has different meanings depending on length and intensity. They are also incredibly impatient, so passing one or two cars at a time on blind curves and at junctions is not uncommon.

More and more cities have traffic lights, though they may be switched off at rush hours and replaced by a traffic policeman. Traffic circles can often be a free-for-all: although vehicles already on the circle have legal priority, others push on if they feel they have been waiting long enough. Lane discipline is almost non-existent (though legally, you are not allowed to undertake), and often where there are only two lanes marked on the road vehicles line up at least four strong. There is no concept of a slow lane or a passing lane, both being used for the same end!

The number of traffic policemen on the main roads is increasing, and they frequently stop drivers for speeding, to check paperwork, and for other traffic offenses, including failing to stop at a pedestrian crossing. In built-up areas the speed limit is 56 kmph (35 mph) and outside towns it is 75 kmph (45 mph). Oncoming vehicles often warn each other of the presence of policemen by flashing their lights. If a driver is penalized for a driving offense, including talking on a cell phone, their driver's license is confiscated and taken to the nearest police station. Irrespective of the driver's residence, he or she must go there to pay the fine and reclaim their license. Drunk driving is illegal, and if caught the driver is taken into police custody. Penalties range from a loss of license and insurance to a spell in prison if the driver has caused a fatal accident.

Over the last decade, Sri Lanka's roads have greatly improved, though many are still poorly lit, potholed, and badly signposted. There are other major hazards too: cattle, dogs, pedestrians, and cyclists seemingly unaware of the road around them, speeding three-wheelers, slow bullock carts, and strange-looking "land masters"—small, belt-driven diesel motors pulling a trailer. The latter two are common forms of transportation in the most rural areas, where other transport services are lacking.

Drivers go through a ritual of circling the wheel with their hands three times and saying a quick prayer before setting off on a long journey, and deposit a few coins in the till when they pass a

Buddhist temple, in the belief that the Buddha will grant them safe passage to wherever they are going. They also adorn their vehicles with religious talismans for further good fortune.

Accidents

Road accidents are common in Sri Lanka and, while most are minor incidents, some end in tragedy. When an accident occurs, onlookers typically crowd around, making unhelpful comments as they survey the damage. Any victims are quickly rushed to the hospital, and chalk is used to mark their positions on the road, as well as the position of the involved vehicles' tires so that they can be moved out of the way if possible. In the meantime, the police are called.

If the scrape is minor, the drivers will usually get out and exchange a few cross words before continuing on their journey. If there is significant damage but no injury, then the cost is either settled through insurance or, if the drivers are not in possession of insurance, worked out between themselves. The increasing number of traffic policemen on the roads has successfully forced most Sri Lankans to buy vehicle insurance of some kind and wear helmets on motorbikes. In general, only drivers without full insurance (where the companies send on-the-spot representatives to survey the damage) need a police report to make an insurance claim.

Bikes and Motorbikes

Bicycles are a popular form of transportation, and it is very common to see two or even three people squeezed onto one bike. Cycling is ideal for the

quieter rural roads; however, on the main roads
cyclists are much more vulnerable to the might of
the buses and trucks that are in no way sensitive to
their presence. While the side of the main road to
the left of either a white or yellow line is designated
for cyclists, other road users rarely recognize this
(and pedestrians share this space, often getting in
the way), so caution should be exercised at all times.

Motorbikes are also very common in Sri Lanka,
and are preferred for their ability to weave quickly in
and out of traffic. They are a more affordable option
than a car and are used to transport the family
about even if that means there are as many as four
or five passengers, including children and babies, on
board. Scooters are available to rent in tourist areas
though you still need to get your license verified
in order to drive them. If you don't validate your
license, whatever insurance comes with the bike
won't be valid.

Pedestrians

While sidewalks do exist in the towns and cities, most are badly constructed and incomplete. Blocked drains result in unpleasant flooding, while cars and rubbish dumped on the sidewalk force pedestrians to walk on roads with a raging torrent of traffic around them. Pedestrians must always remain aware, and be prepared to get out of the way fast if need be. The majority of fatalities from traffic accidents are pedestrians.

Yellow and white pedestrian crossings are found everywhere, especially in urban areas and near schools. While the right of way legally belongs to the pedestrian, and vehicles should stop for them, this is rarely the case as most drivers stop only if they see that someone is already halfway across. When crossing the road you must be bold but sensible; don't cross on a blind curve, and don't rely on your right of way at pedestrian crossings.

Parking

Sri Lankans consider that any large enough space is good enough to park in. However, on main roads in cities—especially Colombo—it is often very difficult to find a legal parking place, especially as many are one-way only and designed to keep traffic moving.

A yellow or white line marked on the road designates an area for cyclists, and/or pedestrians if there is no curb. If the line is yellow, parking is not permitted. If the line is white, you may park, but the vehicle must be completely to the left of the line. Main roads in urban areas are off-limits for parking (though signs telling you this are sporadic) and public car parks are rare, other than at the large city malls. Parking in front of government and military buildings and embassies is forbidden.

If you are visiting a hotel, restaurant, city mall, or even an independent retailer with a car park, there is usually an attendant, smartly dressed in brown or green, who is responsible for the organization of vehicles. He will direct you into a spot and assist you when backing on to the main road on your departure.

LOCAL TRANSPORTATION

The majority of Sri Lankans rely on public transportation, which extensively links even the smallest and most remote rural villages throughout the island. Even those who own motorbikes will take advantage of the many bus routes and more limited train destinations when going on a long journey. Each mode of transportation offers a unique flavor, and can be enjoyed more or less comfortably, depending on the price.

Buses

Buses are the main form of public transportation in Sri Lanka, and as such are commonly crowded. There are three types of bus. The government, or CTB (Central Transport Board), buses are dark red cumbersome Tata vehicles in various states of disrepair; private buses are either large, white-stickered Ashok Leylands or smaller, Japanese, air-conditioned intercity minibuses. The third type are the air-conditioned "luxury" coaches that run up and down the Southern Expressway. Traveling by bus is generally very cheap. Most city bus stations now have signs in English.

Intercity buses are generally the fastest, since they have fewer stops. Apart from the long-distance services, buses rarely follow a structured timetable, but residents know that local buses pass with relative frequency. Traveling by bus is generally a hot and sweaty affair, especially if it is overcrowded. Highly decorated interiors feature electric Buddha images and other religious paraphernalia, while Sinhala or Hindi music often blares loudly from the speakers. The front seats behind the driver are always reserved for the clergy, so if a monk boards anyone sitting there must move. The ones immediately behind these are reserved for pregnant women, and should also be given up if needed. Even in the most crowded situations the conductor will wind his way through the passengers to sell you your ticket.

Taxis

There are a few types of taxi in Sri Lanka, the most characteristic being the ubiquitous motorized three-wheelers, or trishaws. Metered taxis and app-based services such as Uber and local brand PickMe can be found in Colombo and bigger cities, and are efficient and relatively good value. For longer journeys, hiring a car—usually an air-conditioned van—and driver is a good way to travel, since most hotels and guesthouses accommodate drivers who are bringing guests, but it is much more expensive than using local transportation. Drivers in Colombo and the main tourist resorts typically have a good command of English.

Three-wheelers, which will give you your most characteristic and memorable ride in Sri Lanka, are ideal for short trips and are found in abundance throughout the island. Some are basic; others, decked out with glittering accessories, booming stereos, and decorated interiors, are a great source of pride to their owners. By law, all tuk-tuks should be fitted with meters; however in reality this isn't enforced and you usually only find metered tuk-tuks in Colombo. Prices for unmetered tuk-tuks are not fixed, and passengers should agree on a fare, based on the distance and time, before embarking on a trip. Bargaining is expected.

Trains

Traveling by train is often a less stressful experience than by bus and, in most cases, even cheaper. All major routes radiate from Colombo, most of them constructed by the British in the late nineteenth and early twentieth centuries to facilitate the movement of trade and plantation crops. If not overcrowded, trains are a very pleasant way to explore the island, especially the Hill Country, and lines extend east to Batticaloa and Trincomalee and even up to Jaffna.

On trains there are three classes, with first class available only on selected journeys. A few long-distance trains have sleeper carriages. In most cases trains are slower and more prone to delays than buses, but often give the visitor a more enriching cultural experience, with food vendors, beggars singing haunting tunes, and groups of friends dancing in the aisles to the rhythm of a drum. Trains are also where Sri Lankans have the best opportunity to engage you in conversation, and a friendly chat may even lead to an invitation to a Sri Lankan home!

Although you can board any unreserved carriage on the day of travel, booking a reserved seat means you won't have to stand. Tickets become available 30 days prior to travel; however, at busy times of the year trains on popular routes get booked up immediately and tickets are sold on at inflated prices (though it's often hard to track down who has bought them). A really useful resource on train travel in Sri Lanka is www.seat61.com.

Air

Sri Lanka has one well-serviced international airport at Katanayake and a second barely-used international gateway at Mattala, close to Hambantota, named after former president Mahinda Rajapaksa, and built at tremendous expense. There are also an increasing number of small, domestic airports serviced by private Air Taxi operators in key tourist destinations across the island, and many of these airfields—such as Ratmalana, Trincomalee, and Jaffna—are part of Sri Lankan Airforces bases. Private helicopter charters are also possible though they are prohibitively expensive.

WHERE TO STAY

Sri Lanka has a well-developed tourist industry with a great range of accommodation to suit every budget, especially in the most popular resort destinations. While prices in the most exclusive hotels and villas are not usually subject to change, it is possible to negotiate a lower price in most other hotels and guesthouses, especially out of season, when prices can be reduced to a third of their high-season rates. Options include hostels, guesthouses, homestays, boutique hotels, and luxury resorts. Online travel associations such as booking.com and Airbnb.com have a strong presence.

HEALTH

While it is advisable to start planning the health aspects of your trip well in advance your departure, it is reassuring to know that Sri Lanka was declared free from malaria in 2016. However, since mosquitoes carry other diseases such as dengue fever, Japanese encephalitis, and chikungunya, it is important to avoid being bitten. Common precautions include wearing light-colored clothing with long sleeves at night, using a repellent containing deet, and sleeping under a net.

Make sure you are up-to-date with standard vaccinations such as tetanus, diphtheria, polio, and MMR, and covered for water borne diseases such as hepatitis A and typhoid. If you are staying in Sri Lanka for a long period of time, you might also consider being inoculated against rabies. Travel insurance is essential. Keep any hospital or medical receipts so that you can be reimbursed later.

Standards of hygiene in Sri Lanka are relatively good, and while diarrhea is the most common traveler's complaint, it doesn't compare to India's notorious "Delhi belly." Preventive measures include drinking only bottled water, avoiding ice, washing salads in purified water, and avoiding undercooked meat and fish. Stick to freshly cooked, hot food, and avoid anything that looks as if it has been sitting out for a while. As a general rule, the busier the establishment, the better!

Medical care in Sri Lanka is reasonably good. Many doctors have been trained in the West, giving them a good command of English. A free health care system is in place though in reality this is available to Sri Lankans only, except in emergency situations. While there are plenty of private hospitals where you pay for access to the doctor or specialist of your choice, outside Colombo these hospitals aren't usually as well equipped in dealing with emergencies as government hospitals are. The facilities and service in the bigger private hospitals in Colombo are generally very good though relatively expensive. Government hospitals suffer from understaffing and overcrowding. For nonemergencies, family doctors and pharmacies can be found in every town. Appointments are necessary only if you are attending a private hospital or doctor.

SAFETY AND SECURITY
Terrorism
Sri Lanka's twenty-six-year civil war finally came to an end in 2009, while a State of Emergency and the Emergency Regulations were lifted in 2011. Security has relaxed in most areas of the island outside the most contentious areas of the northeast (Mullaitivu, Kilinochi, Mannar, and Vavuniya), and military and police checkpoints are now rare. Operations to clear landmines in former conflict zones are ongoing, so you should heed signs and follow local advice. Political rallies have turned violent on occasion, so it's best to avoid them, particularly at election times.

Given Sri Lanka's recent history, it is always advisable to check with your government's foreign office for the most up-to-date safety advice prior to your arrival.

Crime
Traveling in Sri Lanka is generally very safe. Muggings are uncommon, and violent crime against foreigners is extremely rare. Petty theft is not as rife as in some parts of Asia, but visitors should always take sensible precautions and look after their belongings, especially on crowded buses and trains. Thefts in hotels and guesthouses do occasionally occur, so if there is a safe available it is wise to use it.

Sri Lanka is well known for its con artists. Scams and touting are widespread in a few tourist areas, most notably Colombo's Galle Face Green. Be cautious when approached by "charity collectors," who may be fakes, by anyone selling gems on the street, and by three-wheeler drivers offering to take you to nonexistent elephant festivals. Those who tirelessly attempt to prove their trustworthiness to you should probably be politely avoided.

Women

Sri Lanka is a conservative society, where women are judged by the way they dress and behave. As a rule, the more modestly you dress, and the better you blend in, the less unwanted attention you will receive. Staring is common, and in most cases represents nothing more than curiosity.

Sri Lanka is considered to be one of the safer places for women to travel alone in Asia, and in general men are courteous. However, incidents of harassment by groups of men (ranging from sexually suggestive comments and lewd behavior to physical advances and sexual assaults) are still reported by Western women, including in tourist areas, so you should always take sensible precautions: don't go anywhere unlit at night, and especially not with a stranger. If you are verbally harassed on the street, or when exploring isolated places, it is best to avoid eye contact and walk away. Anger is not a solution, since it is likely to provoke the harassers more.

Sexual harassment has been known to happen on trains and buses, and in markets, under cover of overcrowding, and increasingly in the late night bars and discos of popular tourist areas. Women should beware of stray hands, and politely ignore any unwanted verbal attention. If a man does make an attempt at molestation, draw the attention of other passengers, passersby, or customers to the person responsible. While they can't be relied upon to do anything to assist in this type of situation, letting others know what is happening is usually enough to embarrass and scare off the molester. In such cases it is not only foreign women who are targets, but Sri Lankan women too.

Wildlife

Some wildlife in Sri Lanka is dangerous, and you should particularly be aware of wild elephants (some main roads pass through elephant corridors) and crocodiles around coastal lagoons. Sri Lanka has its fair share of venomous snakes and insects, though these are rarely found in populated areas.

BUSINESS
BRIEFING

The rich diversity of Sri Lanka is well represented
in its business landscape. Small- and medium-
sized enterprises (SMEs) make up the bulk of its
commercial concerns, alongside government-
owned institutions and an increasing number of
multinationals. Sri Lanka has been transformed
from a statist to a market-oriented economy over the
last few decades, with attractive benefits for foreign
investors. International brands have started arriving,
foreign-educated Sri Lankans are returning home
with innovative ideas, and the post-war business
environment as a whole feels upbeat and positive.

While there are many advantages to doing business in Sri Lanka—the island's multiskilled and multilingual labor force are certainly an asset to the country—relatively high taxes, coupled with rigid labor laws that make it almost impossible to fire anyone, are the downsides. While the time taken to set up a business in Sri Lanka has decreased in recent years, the issuing of permits and licenses, especially in construction, entails a lot of red tape, making the process costly and frustratingly lengthy.

The most common Sri Lankan enterprises—public and private limited liability companies—are still the most suitable for foreign investors, along with joint ventures. Representative or liaison offices may also be set up. Sri Lanka has bilateral free trade agreements with India and Pakistan, and various multilateral trade deals, particularly within Asia, including SAFTA (South Asian Free Trade Area).

Many foreign companies register with the Board of Investment (BOI), which might offer advantages such as import duty entitlements. A local partner is not a legal requirement, but it is an advantage to have one, in whom you can trust, as he or she will have inside knowledge of the market and of commercial law, and will be able to cut through the red tape, saving you much time and trouble. However, if you wish to purchase land in Sri Lanka, a local partner is mandatory. Foreigners may only buy freehold properties in Sri Lanka as 49 percent shareholders, excluding apartments above the fourth floor, which foreigners can purchase outright. Leaseholds of up to 99 years are also exempt.

Lawyers in Sri Lanka usually act as a local partner, though be sure to pick a reputable firm. The property's full share value can be fully acquired after 20 years.

The major cities have good facilities in the larger hotels, where business centers are equipped with Wi-Fi or broadband Internet connections, faxes, printing facilities, satellite television, and in some cases audiovisual equipment. The pace of business is slower and more relaxed than in Western countries.

The offices of private businesses are usually open from Monday to Friday from 8:30 a.m. until 5:00 p.m.; some also work until 1:00 p.m. on Saturdays. Smaller businesses might open earlier or finish at the later time of 6:00 p.m., and a few have introduced more flexible working hours, to make it easier for staff to attend to their own personal business and potentially avoid lengthy delays in getting to and from work. Government offices are open only during the week. Muslim businesses may be closed on Fridays between 12 noon and 2:00 p.m. for their weekly prayer session (*Salat al-Jummah*).

THE BUSINESS CULTURE

Regionalism, religion, language, and caste are factors to be aware of when doing business in Sri Lanka, as these will all shape behavioral patterns. In general, all ethnic groups mix and observe harmony in the workplace. Etiquette and approach may need to be modified depending on whom you are addressing and the circumstances. Humor is appreciated, and if used in moderation shows you to be friendly and approachable; however you must be careful not to offend certain groups of people.

People in larger companies and those used to dealing with Western partners will have a good command of English, but if you are dealing with

smaller companies and government departments it may be wise to secure a translator or a trusted third party for both verbal and written communications.

The Importance of Personal Relationships

As is common throughout Asia, the building of long-lasting relationships is the key to business success in Sri Lanka. Sri Lankans like to feel at ease, so it is important to invest time in building a relationship. First impressions are very important, and honesty is highly valued. Trust is also vital, especially because the legal framework of the country cannot always be relied upon to bail you out of a situation, even when there are contracts involved. While trust takes time to earn, a solid grounding results in prompt payments, reliable communication, and a general ease in business partnership. Openness, warmth, respect for the culture, and an ability to fit in are important qualities for the foreign businessperson. Patience is most definitely a virtue.

Contacts

Knowing the right people is very important, and good contacts play a vital role in getting things done. Sometimes the status of a worker's family, their education, connections, or degrees from abroad may be considered more important than their ability to lead, their skills, and dedication. Family businessmen have been known to favor family allegiance and loyalty over competitive skills, and to give young, inexperienced family members prominent roles. Sri Lankans often face pressure from extended family and friends hoping to gain favors from their contacts. Social gain is a strong motivator.

Hierarchy

Not surprisingly, given the traditional social order of the country, hierarchy plays a fundamental role in Sri Lankan business culture, where the boss is very much the boss. Decisions can sometimes be painfully slow in coming, especially in government sector institutions, since they are always referred up to and made at the highest level. The more junior your contact, the longer decisions will take to happen. In many cases initial meetings will take place with middle-ranking personnel, who gather information to pass on to the decision makers. You'll save yourself some time by researching who the best person to speak with would be.

Nonconfrontation

Understanding the Sri Lankan communication style is vital for conducting business. Sri Lankans are nonconfrontational, so harmony should be maintained even when things go wrong. Public expression of emotion is uncommon and a display of impatience, frustration, and annoyance will never work in your favor. "Saving face" is very important throughout Asia, and as pride can sometimes come before business, putting people in awkward positions or under pressure can result in failure. Disagreements can be acerbic and can lead to frustrating and vindictive conduct.

Directness is not usual among Sri Lankans. People have an aversion to saying "no," because of the possibility of causing disappointment or offense, so be aware that noncommittal answers, long pauses, and evasive tactics are very likely to reflect a negative opinion. Most communication goes on between the words rather than within them so you must learn to be intuitive. However frustrating this may be, you should understand that you might not be told directly how others feel or exactly what they want.

BUSINESS ETIQUETTE

First impressions are important, and showing an understanding of Sri Lankan business etiquette is an ideal opportunity to boost your positive image.

Business Dress

Owing to the hot and humid climate, business attire in Sri Lanka is less formal than in the West. While dress codes will vary according to the formality of the business sector, it is important to show respect for your contacts by always being smart—but not in a way that reflects negatively on anyone else. On formal occasions, such as when visiting high government officials and at first meetings, men should wear a lightweight suit; long-sleeved shirts, ties, and pressed trousers are acceptable in more casual situations. Women should always dress modestly and avoid sleeveless blouses, short skirts, and low necklines. Jewelry should be simple and discreet.

Timekeeping

It is important to be punctual for business appointments, as this is also regarded as a sign of respect. You are expected to be on time. Lateness by more than half an hour on the part of Sri Lankans is rare—except when meeting with government officials or functionaries, when you should expect to wait. If you think you might be late, it is polite to call and notify your contact. If it is necessary to cancel a meeting, this should be done at the earliest possible opportunity.

When planning your schedule, leave at least an hour between appointments in case of late starts or meetings that run longer than expected. Travel in Sri Lanka, especially in Colombo, can be hectic and congested, and so you should leave even more time between meetings if you have some distance to go.

Schedules are more relaxed than in the West, as it is generally accepted that things in Sri Lanka take longer to accomplish. It's best not to expect Sri Lankan companies to meet your production or service deadlines, especially when dealing with government institutions, but regular and direct communication with your Sri Lankan counterparts can assist in speeding up the process. It is also important to take the country's many public holidays into account when making your business plans.

Business Cards

Business cards are essential, and are usually exchanged after an initial handshake and formal greeting. They should be presented and received with both hands and studied for a few seconds before being carefully put away. It is important to treat business cards with respect—stuffing them quickly into a pocket would come across as highly disrespectful.

Titles and qualifications are considered important, so these should be added to your business card. Having one side of your card translated into either Sinhala or Tamil is a nice touch if you are regularly doing business in Sri Lanka, but is not essential. It is very cheap to have good cards printed in Sri Lanka.

Gift Giving

Business gifts are acceptable, but should never be offered at the first meeting. Wait for a special occasion, such as the confirmation of a business deal or the completion of a project. Don't be extravagant, or the gift could be misconstrued as a bribe or unfairly pressure the recipient into returning a gift of the same value. Choose something modest—a souvenir of your home country, elegant stationery, an attractive calendar, or something that your company manufactures.

MEETINGS

Appointments should be made in a timely fashion and confirmed closer to the day. It is always good practice to send some background information on your company, the names of those who will be attending, and an outline of the agenda for your meeting in advance. First meetings tend to be the most formal and smart dress is appropriate.

On entering the room you greet the most senior figure first as a mark of respect by shaking hands. Men should wait for a woman to extend her hand first. Use formal forms of address—titles are important to Sri Lankans—and don't use first names until you are invited to. If your contact has no professional title, just use Mr., Mrs., or Miss with the person's first name or surname.

Since good business relationships are key in Sri Lanka, it is important to introduce yourself and engage in some polite conversation at the start of meetings. You should expect a lot of small talk before business is discussed; use this time to get to know your contacts. Good topics to discuss are family, your country, cricket, and your impressions of Sri Lanka. If you have met your contact before you could ask after his or her family. Men and women are equally open to conversation.

Small talk has its advantages; since Sri Lankan contract law can be rather sketchy, personal rather than contractual relationships are often what bind businesses together. Sri Lankans feeling comfortable with you on a personal level will result in a well-grounded and long-lasting business relationship, even in times of trouble.

Because business in Sri Lanka is hierarchically organized, the decision makers do not always attend meetings. Initial meetings will typically be attended by middle-ranking personnel who will collate the information to pass on to the decision maker. Their opinion is important, as they will be the ones representing you to the higher authorities, and so making a good first impression is vital.

In meetings expect to be served highly sweetened tea with cookies. Don't be put off if your meeting is interrupted by other business, or if someone is called to the telephone, as this sometimes has to happen and should not be interpreted as rude. Always remain polite and friendly throughout.

It is very important to follow up your meeting with telephone calls to sustain the relationships that have been forged and check that the business is going ahead as discussed.

PRESENTATIONS

Presentations are common in Sri Lanka, and technical equipment is now quite sophisticated. Certainly the business premises in many of the island's top hotels are first class. Presentations are conducted in much the same way as in the West, although they have a higher chance of being interrupted.

In presenting your ideas, it is important to have a relaxed and friendly approach. Explain, as clearly as you can, your vision, and how you plan to achieve your goals. Clarity at this stage will help to avoid misunderstandings and will make the later part of your job easier.

Your presentation should be concise and easily understandable. Since the decision maker may not be present, you want to make sure that your Sri Lankan counterpart is able to relay your vision and goals clearly to the higher authorities. When dealing with smaller companies and government institutions, it always helps to have some presentation materials, and perhaps the main points, translated into either Sinhalese or Tamil for local consumption.

It is recommended that you bring your own laptop with you, but other equipment should be provided. Calling in advance to find out what equipment is available is advisable if you are planning on giving a particularly technical display. How much time you will need will depend on the nature of the topic, but try not to exceed one hour. Remember that the level of seniority of the person you are presenting to gives an indication of the time that you have; people in authority tend to have less time, so concentrate on getting to the point quickly. If there are interruptions, wait until you have their full attention again before continuing.

NEGOTIATIONS

In negotiations, remember that Sri Lankans are not direct in their demands and that they don't like saying the word "no." Vague and noncommittal comments often hint at a negative response. It is important to learn to read between the lines.

You should be clear from the start about your aims, requirements, expectations, and conditions. Take minutes or document every discussion and agreement for future reference. Negotiations can be slow, especially in the early stages and if you have to do the groundwork with middle managers. You'll only be able to seal the deal with the decision makers, so try to get to meet them face-to-face if you can, to discuss your aims and concerns directly.

When negotiating with Sri Lankans, avoid high-pressure tactics. Being confrontational or forceful will have a negative effect, while criticisms and disagreements should only be voiced in the most diplomatic manner. Politeness is the key to clinching deals.

Business decisions may be based as much on faith, intuition, and feeling as on statistical data. Sinhalese and Tamil people believe in astrology, and are guided by their belief in a higher force that controls most aspects of day-to-day life. Astrologers may be consulted to gain clearance for new business premises or to establish a good or auspicious time to start a new project. Many firmly believe that any outcome, good or bad, is a result of *karma*. It is wise to respect these cultural values, and not show any frustration if they cause delays. If the negotiating process is successful, and you have a deal, it is appropriate to acknowledge this with a celebratory dinner, drink, or gift.

CONTRACTS

Sri Lankan commercial law is largely statutory. While it was codified before independence in 1948 and still reflects many aspects of the British law of the time, amendments have mostly kept pace with successive legal changes in the UK. The Board of Investment Law, the Intellectual Property Act, the Companies Act, and the Consumer Affairs Authority Act are just some of the important legal enactments that regulate Sri Lankan commercial affairs. Civil law is predominantly Roman-Dutch.

A contract will give your deal legality in Sri Lanka, but unfortunately, if things do go wrong, the court system cannot be always relied upon.

Resolving disputes in the courts is time-consuming, since procedures allow for one party to prolong the case indefinitely. Many companies prefer to resolve disputes out of court and include an arbitration clause in their contracts. In any case, it is important to be represented by a good legal team.

Contracts are presented in either English or Sinhalese, and while it is very important that you instruct your lawyer to check a contract before you sign it, the lawyer does not need to be present when you do so. You are expected to honor the terms of a contract once they are agreed on, and you should make frequent follow-up calls to ensure proper compliance.

DEALING WITH THE GOVERNMENT

The government exercises a great deal of control over businesses in Sri Lanka, and many administrative appointments are politically motivated. Having the right contacts politically—the higher the better—is a significant advantage. The Board of Investment (BOI) is a government institution specifically set up as a one-stop shop for current and potential foreign investors.

A bureaucratic and onerous tax system combined with rigid labor laws weighs heavily on all businesses operating in Sri Lanka. The tax system is considered a major constraint, and the difficulty in complying with it has created an environment conducive to corruption. The island ranks well below other South Asian countries on the ease of paying taxes (especially in relation to foreign companies), making it less competitive in attracting investment. While the Sri Lankan authorities have begun to simplify procedures by reducing the number of tariffs, steps, and costs, companies still have to spend a great deal of time with tax officials, make many payments a year, and forfeit a large percentage of their profits. The result is significant tax evasion: less than 7 percent of the country's labor force and formal institutions pay tax.

On April 1, 2018, however, new tax laws came into effect under the guidance of the IMF designed to improve the tax system and to help improve the weak financial performance of state-owned enterprises.

CORRUPTION

Sri Lanka has its fair share of corruption problems. High-level corruption, characterized by cronyism and nepotism, is frequently discussed in the Sri Lankan media; however, there have never been any major cases resulting in a conviction. Corruption in Sri Lanka is still at a moderate level compared to other Asian countries (ranking below India and above Pakistan, Thailand, and Bangladesh in Transparency International's 2017 Corruption Perception Index); however, it is still identified by many companies as one of the major constraints on business operations, especially by investors in large projects and companies seeking government procurement contracts.

Bribery is common in Sri Lanka, so companies operating businesses there risk encountering corrupt practices. Investors should exercise caution when seeking local persons to facilitate transactions on their behalf, to avoid recruiting potentially corrupt agents. A Bribery Commission investigates charges of corruption.

The public sector is perceived to be the most corrupt sphere, where bribes are offered to obtain necessary permits and licenses. Those working in this sector consider their salaries to be low and regard bribes as a way of supplementing their incomes. Loopholes in the law are also a contributory factor. However, despite the fact that it's common practice, there are many employees who would be deeply offended if they were to be offered a bribe.

WOMEN IN BUSINESS

Sri Lankan businesspeople are accustomed to dealing with foreign women in managerial positions, and, depending on the industry, Sri Lankan women are often their counterparts. Gender equality is enshrined in Sri Lankan law, and women should be treated equally in the workplace. Those at the higher levels can expect to receive the same amount of respect as their male counterparts, especially in the corporate and private sectors.

The first country in the world to have a female prime minister, Sri Lanka set the standard to some extent, and women are taking on more authoritative roles; however it is still much more common for a man to be the decision maker in a large company.

SOCIALIZING

Entertaining in a business context, while important, is quite modest in Sri Lanka. Sri Lankans are very hospitable, and many enjoy getting out of the office to talk business in a less formal setting. Unless you know your hosts quite well, it is unlikely that you will be invited to their home. An invitation to a business associate's home, therefore, is a clear sign of acceptance, and should not be refused.

Socializing mainly takes place in social clubs, restaurants, cafés, and bars, some of which are located in Colombo's more prestigious five-star hotels. It is unlikely that spouses will join you for a business lunch or dinner. Remember that many women in Sri Lanka refrain from drinking alcohol, so if there are to be women in the group it is advisable to choose a café or a restaurant rather than a bar as a meeting place, so as not to put them in an uncomfortable situation. Similarly, be aware of a person's cultural heritage. Muslims, for example, may not drink, and never eat pork.

Much of the business talk will go on during and after the meal rather than before, since this is the time to develop your relationship with small talk. Whoever has offered the invitation for the dinner or drinks is usually responsible for paying the bill, but it is important to reciprocate and not take anyone's hospitality for granted.

chapter **nine**

COMMUNICATING

LANGUAGE

While Sri Lanka is a trilingual nation, there are only two official languages—Sinhala and Tamil. Sinhala is spoken by around 74 percent of the population, most of whom are Sinhalese, while Tamil is spoken by around 18 percent. English is classed as a link language and is also widely spoken, often as a second language, and was the official language of Ceylon until shortly after independence. The Sri Lankan Creole Malay language is spoken in the homes of the Malay population.

Language is a controversial subject. The passing of the "Sinhala Only" law in 1956, demoting the Tamil

language and thus excluding Tamils from taking up government positions, was one of the major underlying causes of the civil war. While Tamil was reinstated as an official language in 1988, the topic is still politically sensitive.

Sinhala is an Indo-Aryan language, spoken only in Sri Lanka. It evolved, influenced by successive waves of settlers and colonists, from the language Prince Vijaya and his entourage brought to the island in the fifth century BCE. Tamil, and to a lesser extent Portuguese, Dutch, Malay, and English have all contributed to it. Its closest linguistic relative is the Maldivian Dhivehi. While Sinhala is spoken island-wide, it has little impact in the Tamil-dominated north and east. Written and colloquial Sinhala differ markedly, and the beautiful, curvilinear script is comprised of forty-seven characters.

Tamil is an ancient language spoken predominantly in southern India, as well as in Malaysia and Singapore. It belongs to the southern branch of the Dravidian language and was brought to Sri Lanka by South Indian invaders from the third century BCE. Sri Lankan Tamil is a distinct dialect, having over the years acquired its own accent and vocabulary, spoken widely in the north and east, and less so in Colombo and the Hill Country. The Tamil script, while also curvilinear, is characterized more by rectangular shapes than the Sinhala script.

Sri Lankan English is unique, in that it has developed its own expressions, words, and idiosyncrasies of spelling, grammar, and punctuation. Since independence and its cessation as a national language, it has evolved to incorporate more Sinhalese vocabulary and grammatical conventions: for example, a "hotel" can mean a roadside restaurant, a "saloon" a hair salon, while "short eats" are snacks. The use of the tag word "no?" at the end of sentences such as "You're coming back, no?" and the frequent omission of the definite article (the) are typical characteristics of Sri Lankan English.

Muslims speak Tamil peppered with Arabic words, although those living in the south and west of the island may also speak Sinhala. English is typically the mother tongue of the Burghers, while it is the second language for many Sri Lankans living in cities and tourist areas. Westernized urbanites and bilingual Sinhala speakers often combine English words and phrases with their own language ("Singlish"), curiously dipping in and out of both as they speak. All official signs, banknotes, and government papers, are printed in the three languages, while many businesses and shops have signs in Sinhala and English, Tamil and English, or all three, depending on their location.

While you can easily travel around Sri Lanka speaking only English, it is a good idea to learn some Sinhala (or Tamil if your travels take you to the north and east), as Sri Lankans will deeply appreciate your efforts at communication. Sinhala is easier to learn than Tamil, and you will encounter it more commonly on a daily basis. Many English teachers offer private Sinhala language lessons to foreigners. Making mistakes is fine, and while some people may be amused when a foreigner speaks their language, you shouldn't be put off, since this usually just represents surprise. The next reaction will be to talk to you to find out how much you really know!

Sri Lankans often ask, "What to do?" when they are in an unfamiliar or uncomfortable situation. This can be a rhetorical question while they search for a possible solution, or can approximate to a Western shrug of the shoulders. It is also said in consolation, or in response to something where it is obvious that no solution can be given, and in these cases simply means, "Nothing can be done."

GESTURES AND BODY LANGUAGE

The most characteristic nonverbal form of communication in Sri Lanka is the famous head waggle. In conversation, someone will often signal assent, agreement, or understanding by moving the head from side to side, and at the same time slightly up and down, and saying "*Ha*." At first sight a foreigner might interpret this as shaking the head in disagreement, but on closer inspection it can be seen that the Sri Lankan action is in fact very different.

To beckon someone toward them, a Sri Lankan will hold one arm outstretched and, with the palm facing down, move the fingers inward. It is considered impolite to point at someone using the index finger, so gestures of moving the head or raising the eyebrows in the direction of the subject are commonly used. Hand gestures are often used to highlight a point.

Sri Lankans are less aware of personal space than people in the West, so conversations between two friends are often carried out in very close proximity to each other. Lines are free-for-alls where you have to hold your ground. The opposite is true when a Sri Lankan is speaking to his superior, where the greater the social divide, the greater the personal space maintained.

THE MEDIA

The Sri Lanka media is trilingual. Newspapers, television, and radio stations come in Sinhala, Tamil, and English, and are either state or privately owned. The extensive English-language media comprises a selection of dailies, including *The Island*, *Daily News*, *Daily Mirror*, and *The Nation*, as well as a few weekly newspapers such as the *Sunday Observer*, *Sunday Times*, and *Sunday Leader*. Sinhala and Tamil newspapers are as numerous and enjoy wide circulations in their homelands, reflecting the high literacy rate of the population. Newspapers are available from newsstands and independent retailers alongside a growing range of travel, lifestyle, fashion, and business-oriented magazines. Newspapers have online editions while roak.lk, an online media platform established in 2014, reports on current affairs, business, technology, lifestyle, and culture.

Local television channels broadcast almost entirely in Sinhala and Tamil, although there are some English-language news channels and radio stations. Satellite television is increasingly widespread; foreign broadcasters such as the BBC, CNN, and Al-Jazeera offer an international perspective on events both in the country and worldwide.

During the Rajapaksa era and the final years of the civil war, press freedom in Sri Lanka was rated as one of the worst in the democratic world, ranking 167 out of 173 countries, according to Reporters Without Borders. Media institutions and individuals critical of the regime and their practices were often threatened, and as many as forty-four journalists have been killed since 2004. Although the situation has improved in the postwar years under President Sirisena, and censorship laws have been relaxed, the government still maintains a degree of media control and influence—both the *Daily News* and the *Sunday Observer* are state-owned. In 2018 Sri Lanka's press freedom ranking rose to 137.

SERVICES
Telephone
The Sri Lankan telecommunications industry was one of the first in South Asia to launch 3G mobile phones. International calls in Sri Lanka are relatively inexpensive and you'll find communication bureaus offering IDD calls, fax, photocopying, and e-mail services in almost every town and village. Most Sri Lankans (or at least households) now have a mobile phone, and many of these are smartphones.

Sri Lankan cell phone networks are based on GSM and CDMA technology. Most UK, Australian, and New Zealand cell phones work well in Sri

Lanka, although those from the USA that aren't tri-band might not. The five main cell phone networks are Dialog, Mobitel, Etisalat, Hutch, and Airtel. If you plan on being in Sri Lanka for a while, it's generally cheaper to pick up a local SIM card (prepaid or contract), which can be bought at the airport or at any phone shop around the island, though your phone will need to be "unlocked" first to accept a foreign SIM card. This can be done locally. Prepaid cards are available at nearly every communications bureau—look out for which company's sign and stickers emblazon the shop.

Fixed telephone lines can be costly to install, and waiting lists are long so many Sri Lankans rely on cell phones. The state-run Sri Lanka Telecom has the majority market share.

Mail

While domestic mail in Sri Lanka is notoriously slow and erratic, airmail is usually very reliable. Since mail might be opened at customs, or lost or damaged in transit, it is a good idea to register it or send it by EMS Speed Post—a faster airmail service that takes three or four days to reach Europe and less than a week to reach the USA. International couriers FedEx and DHL both have offices in Colombo and other major cities. Businesses in Colombo and across the island prefer to hand deliver important documents directly to their client's offices wherever possible.

Sri Lanka has a good network of post offices, reaching even the smallest rural villages. Money orders, payment of utility bills, and fines for automobile traffic offenses are other services handled at post offices. Mailmen deliver mail on foot, or by bicycle—tinkling their bell from the roadside outside a house to signal their arrival. Mailboxes on the streets are not always regularly emptied, so it is best to take your mail to a post office. If sending a package, you must take it unsealed, as the contents have to be checked.

Major post offices operate longer hours than smaller ones and are open from 7:00 a.m. to 8:00 p.m. or 9:00 p.m. during the week and until 4:00 p.m. on Saturday. Smaller branches usually close by mid-afternoon.

When addressing mail always include the postcode. A full list of postcodes can be found on the Sri Lanka Post Website (www.slpost.gov.lk). If sending mail to someone who is not a permanent resident at the address, send it c/o the name of someone who is.

Internet

Internet access is widely available and nearly every hotel, guesthouse, hostel, and restaurant offers free Wi-Fi. As such, Internet cafés aren't as widespread as they once were. Popular Internet Service Providers include Dialog 4G (for prepaid broadband) and Sri Lanka Telecom (SLT), which offer a range of monthly packages.

CONCLUSION

Sri Lanka is a country of great contrast and diversity, where people are genuinely friendly, welcoming, and warm. Despite economic disparity, practicing different religions, and hailing from a range of ethnic backgrounds, all Sri Lankans share a great respect for family, home, and friendship, and pride in their beautiful island. Their recent history has been turbulent, but they have also shown great resilience in the face of the 2004 tsunami and the civil war.

Trust takes some time to earn, and although tempers may flare if grievances are left to simmer, they are quickly calmed through dialogue. Sri Lankans are characteristically indirect, but we know that this comes not from evasiveness or discourtesy, but from a wish not to disappoint, cause embarrassment, or lose face. Politeness, respect, a genuine attempt to understand their culture, and open acceptance of the island's relaxed pace, are the keys to gaining acceptance in turn by Sri Lankans and to having an enjoyable visit.

Further Reading

Amirthalingam, G. *Customs and Cultures of Sri Lanka*. London: A & S Books, 2003.

De Silva, K.M. *A History of Sri Lanka*. Colombo: Vijitha Yapa Publications, 2005.

Deraniyagala, Sonali. *Wave: A Memoir of Life after the Tsunami*. London: Virago, 2013.

Dissanayake, J.B. *Say it in Sinhala*. Colombo: Lake House Investments, 1993.

Gimlette, John. *Elephant Complex: Travels in Sri Lanka*. London: riverrun, 2016.

Meyler, Michael. *A Dictionary of Sri Lankan English*. Colombo: Michael Meyler, 2007.

Muller, Carl. *The Jam Fruit Tree*. Gurugram: PRHI, 2000.

Ondaatje, Christoper. *Woolf in Ceylon*. New York: HarperCollins Publications, 2005.

Ondaatje, Michael: *Running in the Family*. New York: Vintage, 1993.

Ondaatje, Michael. *Anil's Ghost:* New York: Vintage, 2001.

Subramanian, Samanth. *This Divided Island. Stories from the Sri Lankan war.* New York: Thomas Dunne Books, 2015.

Tambiah, Stanley J. *Buddhism Betrayed? Religion, Politics and Violence in Sri Lanka*. Chicago: University of Chicago Press, 1992.

Thomas, Gavin. *The Rough Guide to Sri Lanka*. London: Rough Guides, 2018.

Woolfe, Leonard. *The Village in the jungle*. London: Eland, 2016.

Index